Innkeepers' Finest Breakfasts

The American Bed and Breakfast Association's

Blue Ribbon Breakfast Recipe

Contest Winners

Dependable, delicious recipes from AB&BA's breakfast recipe contest; innkeepers' funniest kitchen moments; and preparation tips to save time, money, and make breakfast special.

Jessica Bennett

April Haven Press

Innkeepers' Finest Breakfasts

Copyright 1994 by Jessica Bennett

All rights reserved. No part of this book may be used or reproduced in any manner whatsoever without written permission except in the case of brief quotations embodied in critical articles or reviews.

April Haven Press
Publisher

Jessica Bennett	**Wendy Van Nest**	**Carol Curry**
Author	Illustrations	Layout

Printed in The United States of America
by BookCrafters, Fredericksburg, Virginia
ISBN 0-9638785-0-6

For ordering additional copies write:
Jessica Bennett
Box 3048
Crofton, MD 21114

I wish to express my special thanks to the bed and breakfasts who contributed recipes for the contest; Sarah Sonke of the American Bed and Breakfast Association for her help; my husband, Les Bennett, for his encouragement; Barbara Crispin for editing; and the test cooks and judges for their careful work.

Test Cooks and Judges

Martha McGovern	Joyce Brawner
Maureen Berger	Denise Pizzino
Connie Webb	Shirley Brooks
Pat Baugher	Barbara Meager
Peter Tabatsko	Pam Connolly
Heather Ross	Roni Starkey
Edward Crafts	Barbara Crispin
Elizabeth Bennett	Yvonne Gurney

TABLE OF CONTENTS
Make Ahead Recipes identified with an *.

Main Dishes

Westway's Favorite Mexican Casserole............3
Keeper of the Inn Pinto Beans *.......................3
Baked Apple Oatmeal *....................................4
Make Ahead Breakfast Eggs *..........................5
Breakfast Quiche Casserole *..........................6
Windyledge Potato Sausage Bake....................7
Orange Oatmeal Pie...8
Lobster Omelet..9
Shrimp and Brie Scrambled Eggs...................10
Farmer's Breakfast...11
Featherbed Eggs *...12
Ellen's Breakfast Casserole *.........................12
Ranchers' Eggs..13
Baked Deviled Eggs *....................................14
Eggs Hersey *..15
Fresh Vegetable Frittata.................................16
Garden Vegetable Strata *.............................17
Ham and Potato Pie Supreme........................18
Westway's Southwestern Souffle...................19
Tostada Quiche Del Rey *..............................20
Stuffed Tuna Bread *.....................................21
D B's Hot Chicken Salad *.............................22
Breakfast Flan *...23
Kaiserschmarrn..24
Plum Cheese Blintzes....................................25
German Pancake...26
Best Ever Granola *.......................................27
Breakfast Granola *.......................................28
Honey Granola *..29

Fruit Dishes

Virginia Apple Puff...33
Honey Minted Grapes *.................................34
Raspberry-Banana Trifle *..............................35
Rhubarb Rollups..36
The Cottage Breakfast Pie *..........................37
Kiwi Pizza *...38
Geranium Leaf Sorbet *.................................39
Princely Peach Soup *...................................40
Chilled Strawberry Soup *..............................41

Tropical Fruit Salad..42
Grapefruit in Blackberry Sauce.......................43
Apple Crunch *..44
Swedish Apple Pie...45
Baked Apples *..46
Oven Fried Apples...46
Baked Stuffed Pears *...................................47
Pear Surprise..48
Maple Poached Pears...................................49
Glazed Bananas..50
Banana Split Supreme...................................50
Winter Windfall *..51
Hot Fruit Compote...52

Muffins

Raspberry-Blueberry Surprise Muffins..........55
Raspberry Bran Muffins................................56
Blueberry-Boothbay Muffins.........................57
Blueberry Lemon Muffins..............................58
Blueberry Orange Muffins.............................59
Berry Streusel Muffins..................................60
Refrigerated Apricot Bran Muffins *..............61
Apricot Muffins...62
Apricot-Almond Pound Cake Muffins...........63
Pumpkin Pecan Muffins................................64
Green Apple Muffins.....................................65
Banana Muffins...66
Bran Muffins with Maple Syrup.....................67
Mika's Marvelous Muffins.............................68
Chocolate Chip Muffins................................69

Quick Breads

Ann's Poppy Seed Bread..............................73
Lemon Poppy Seed Bread............................74
Poppy Seed Bread..75
Chocolate Applesauce Bread........................76
Emily's Banana Bread...................................77
Grandmom's Banana Bread..........................78
Dried Fruit Cream Scones............................79
Berry Cobbler...80
Western Cowboy Baking Powder
  Biscuit Mix *...81

TABLE OF CONTENTS con't.
Make Ahead Recipes identified with an *.

Peach Yogurt Bread 82
Gay's Banana Orange Muffin Cake 83
Kathy's Graham Bread 84
Saffron Buns 85

Coffee Cakes
Apple Bundt Cake 89
Breakfast Apple Cake 90
Viennese Crescent Ring 91
Pumpkin Coffee Cake 92
Fresh Fruit Breakfast Cake 93
Grandma Flick's Blueberry Coffee Cake 94
Raspberry Cream Cheese Coffee Cake 95

Yeast Breads
Applebutter Sweet Rolls * 99
Mary Yoder's Yummy Cinnamon Rolls 100
Sour Cream Bread Roll * 101
Refrigerator Coffee Cake 102
Colonial Bread From 1650 103
Oatmeal Apple Bread 104
Quick Egg Bread 105
Bread for the Busy Innkeeper 106
Linda's Bread 107

Pancakes and Waffles
Four Berry Pancakes 111
Betty's Buttermilk Pancakes
 A La Strawberries 112
Lemon Ricotta Pancakes 113
Bavarian Pancake 114
Taylor's Store Whole-Grain Pancakes 115
Whole Grain Pancakes 116

Apple Walnut Whole Wheat Pancakes 117
Colonial Newport Jonnycakes 118
Banana Buttermilk Buckwheat Pancakes ... 119
Cottage Crepes * 120
Lemon Poppy Seed Waffles 121
Norwegian Waffles 122
Whole Wheat Waffles 123

French Toast
Blushing Rose's French Toast * 127
Country French Toast 128
Sunny Pines Surprise Toast 129
Baked French Toast * 130
Peaches and Cream French Toast * 131
Dunscroft's Own Best French Toast Ever .. 131
Plumy French Toast 132
Ricotta-Stuffed French Toast 133
Stuffed French Toast 134
Heidi's Stuffed French Toast * 135

Condiments and Beverages
Cinnamon Honey Butter * 139
Honey Pecan Butter * 140
Strawberry Butter * 141
Merry Berry Syrup * 141
Cherry Sauce * 142
Rhubarb Sauce * 143
Rhubarb Raspberry Sauce * 143
Cranberry Conserve * 144
Apple Conserve * 145
Rhubarb Marmalade * 146
Apple-Berry Tea * 147
Hot Mulled Cider * 147

Main Dishes

WESTWAY'S FAVORITE MEXICAN CASSEROLE   Serves 6
MAIN DISH BLUE RIBBON BREAKFAST WINNER !!

1/2 cup chopped onion	2 eggs
2 tablespoons butter or margarine	1 cup half and half (or milk)
8 ounces tomato sauce	6 corn tortillas
4 ounces diced green chilies	3/4 pound Monterey Jack cheese, shredded
1/2 teaspoon celery salt	8 ounces sour cream
1/4 teaspoon pepper	4 ounces cheddar cheese, shredded

Saute the onion in butter until it is transparent. Add the tomato sauce, chilies, celery salt, and pepper. Simmer for 5 minutes and remove the pan from the heat. Beat the eggs and mix in the half and half. Stir the egg mixture into the tomato mixture. Quarter the tortillas and layer one-third of the tortillas, one-third of the tomato mixture, and one-third of the Jack cheese in a large casserole. Repeat the layers three times. Carefully frost the casserole with sour cream and sprinkle with cheddar cheese. Bake at 350 degrees for 35-45 minutes.

Darrell's Keeper of the Inn Pinto Beans recipe makes a good side dish to the above casserole.

KEEPER OF THE INN PINTO BEANS

3 cups dried pinto beans, washed and cleaned
1/2 cup oil
4 cloves garlic, chopped
1/2 teaspoon pepper
2 tablespoons powdered red chili
1/2 pound salt pork, diced
1 medium onion, quartered
1 tablespoon sugar

Soak the beans in water to cover them and refrigerate overnight. Drain and cover generously with fresh water and add all the other ingredients. Boil for 1 to 1 1/2 hours, skimming the top occasionally and adding more water as needed to keep the beans moist. Mash the beans slightly and cook for another 30 minutes. The beans may be served at this point or may simmer all day for the fullest flavor. Add water when necessary. Add salt to taste just before serving. This freezes well.

Westways "Private" Resort Inn
Darrell Trapp
P.O. Box 41624
Phoenix, Arizona 85080
telephone: (602) 582-3868

BAKED APPLE OATMEAL

Serves 2

MAKE-AHEAD BLUE RIBBON BREAKFAST WINNER !!

4 cups old fashioned oats
1 cup brown sugar
1 teaspoon salt
2 tablespoons cinnamon
2 cups raisins
3 cups nonfat dry milk
2 cups chopped nuts

Combine the above ingredients and store in an airtight container.

In the morning, combine the following in a 12 ounce bean pot and bake uncovered for 30 to 35 minutes in a 350 degree oven. Serve with milk. Makes enough for 2 servings.

1 cup dry mix
1 teaspoon butter
1/4 large apple peeled and chopped
1 cup boiling water

Sandlake Country Inn
Margo Underwood
8505 Galloway Road
Cloverdale, OR 97112
telephone: (503) 965-6745

The Underwoods recall a harried moment: "It's Sunday morning. Ten guests. Rooms full. We have prepared a buffet style continental breakfast of huge bowls of fresh fruit, vanilla yogurt, and homemade granola. The first couple comes down. The gentleman is a 6'6" health enthusiast. He proceeds to eat all, yes, ALL of everything. When I walked in to check on them, his wife smiled and said, 'Isn't he cute?'"

Because of this incident, the Underwoods now layer the same ingredients in wine goblets, call it a breakfast parfait, and serve one to each guest.

This make-ahead recipe, the judges concluded, is unusually good. It is delicious, convenient, wholesome, and filling. A partially covered casserole could be used instead of a bean pot, although the bean pot makes the presentation of this dish special.

MAKE AHEAD BREAKFAST EGGS Serves 8

1 dozen eggs
2 tablespoons butter
1/2 cup milk
1 cup plain yogurt or sour cream
10 slices bacon
1 cup shredded Cheddar cheese

Melt the butter and scramble the eggs and milk until soft set. When the eggs have cooled slightly, add the yogurt or sour cream. Spread the egg mixture into a buttered 9" X 9" baking pan. Crumble cooked bacon over the eggs. Sprinkle shredded Cheddar cheese over the top. Cover the pan with foil and refrigerate overnight.

In the morning, bake covered for 30 minutes at 325 degrees. Remove the foil and bake 5 to 10 minutes longer until the cheese is melted. This will keep well on a warming tray for one to two hours.

Bed and Breakfast of Waterville
Stanley and Carol Sambora
211 White Street
Waterville, NY 13480
telephone: (315) 841-8295

BREAKFAST QUICHE CASSEROLE   Serves 16 to 18

1 pound Italian sausage
1 medium onion, diced
1 green pepper, diced
20 eggs, beaten
4 tablespoons milk or cream
2 or 3 red tomatoes, diced
1/2 teaspoon oregano
1/2 teaspoon basil
1/2 teaspoon ground pepper
1 cup grated cheese

Saute the sausage until brown and drain off the fat. Saute the onion and green pepper. Mix all the ingredients in a large bowl and pour into a large buttered casserole dish. Sprinkle the grated cheese over the top.

At this point the casserole may be covered and refrigerated overnight, if desired.

Bake at 350 degrees for one hour. Serve immediately. "Beautiful, hot and bubbly out of the oven!"

This can also be prepared using a half pound sweet sausage and a half pound hot sausage.

The recipe can be halved if a smaller amount is needed.

Dunscroft by-the-Sea Inn and Cottage
Alyce and Wally Cunningham
24 Pilgrim Road
Harwich Port, MA 02646
telephone: (508) 432-0810

To make breakfast preparation easier, the Cunningham's advise, "Get up early enough! Plan the menu ahead, at least mentally, the night before. Select easy, yet delicious recipes. Don't pick recipes with 15-20 ingredients. Budget your time."

Alyce puts out a large silver platter lined with a lace doily and filled with fresh fruit. She serves muffins in an attractive basket, lined with a colorful napkin. She prefers to serve the main dish in a chafing dish in the center of the table and presents cut up fruit in a footed trifle glass dish.

For those guests who want breakfast-to-go at 6:00 A.M., there is always cereal. Yogurt, milk, juice, and fresh fruit are in the guest refrigerator. There is bread and a toaster which guests may use. Coffee is put on a timer which can be set earlier when needed.

The judges thought this would make a good brunch dish as well as a spicy breakfast entree.

WINDYLEDGE POTATO SAUSAGE BAKE   Serves 6 to 8

6 medium potatoes
1/4 cup melted butter
1 medium onion, chopped
1/2 teaspoon minced garlic
1 teaspoon basil
1 teaspoon summer savory
12 ounces bulk pork sausage
salt and pepper to taste
3/4 cup herbed stuffing mix, divided
1/4 cup butter, melted
1 cup milk
8 ounces cheddar cheese, shredded

Preheat the oven to 350 degrees. Peel, slice, and boil the potatoes. Melt 1/4 cup butter in a frying pan and saute the onion and garlic. Add the basil, savory, and 4 tablespoons herbed stuffing mix. Set aside. Fry the sausage on medium heat and drain off the fat. Add the onion mixture to the sausage. Drain the potatoes and stir the potatoes to break them into smaller pieces. Stir the potatoes into the sausage mixture. Salt and pepper to taste. Place the mixture in a sprayed 9" X 13" oven proof dish. Mix the cheese, melted butter, and milk with the remaining stuffing mix and sprinkle over the top. Bake for 40 minutes.

> Windyledge Bed and Breakfast
> Dick and Susan Vogt
> Hatfield Road
> Hopkinton, NH 03229
> telephone: (603) 746-4054

The potato sausage bake was judged to be a very good recipe that most guests would like very much. "Although it is not an elegant dish, it is very hearty and filling," commented a judge. "It cut into nicer servings after it had cooled for 20 minutes.

ORANGE OATMEAL PIE
Serves 6

3/4 cup milk
3 beaten eggs
1/2 cup orange juice
1/4 cup sugar (optional)
1/2 cup quick-cook oatmeal
2 tablespoons melted butter
1 teaspoon orange rind
1/8 teaspoon salt
9" unbaked pie shell (optional)

Mix the first eight ingredients well and pour the mixture into the pie shell or a buttered quiche dish. Bake at 350 degrees for 35 to 40 minutes or until set. Let the pie stand a few minutes. Serve it in wedges and top each slice with yogurt or cream, if desired.

Low Cholesterol Modifications:
3/4 cup skim milk
egg beaters or 3 egg whites
2 tablespoons margarine

> Blushing Rose Bed and Breakfast
> Ellen and Bucky Laufersweiler
> 11 William Street
> Hammondsport, NY 14840
> telephone: (607) 569-3402

Like many innkeepers, the Laufersweilers have found that the microwave comes in handy. "When the middle of my dish is not done, thank goodness for that wonderful micro!"

For large groups, a real morning time saver is to "prepare the main dish casserole the night before and refrigerate it."

The judges thought this recipe was surprisingly good and out of the ordinary.

LOBSTER OMELET

Serves 2 to 3

Omelet:
6 eggs
1/2 cup cream
3 tablespoons grated parmesan cheese
1 teaspoon parsley (optional)
salt and pepper to taste

Filling:
1/2 cup freshly caught and boiled lobster meat
2/3 cup shredded Monterey Jack cheese
fresh zucchini microwaved until tender (optional)

Whisk the omelet ingredients on high in the blender for 30 seconds. Pour equal amounts of the egg mixture into each side of a heated, buttered, folding omelet pan. Cover the pan with foil and cook slowly until the eggs are half set. Tip the pan and slightly push the egg mixture with a spatula allowing the uncooked portion to run into the pan. Recover the pan with foil and repeat.

When the egg mixture is set, add the filling.

Close the omelet pan and cook. The omelet will puff like a souffle.

This recipe can be adapted to an omelet skillet.

Atlantic Seal Bed and Breakfast
Capt. Thomas Ring and Gaila Ring
P.O. Box 146 25 Main Street
South Freeport, Maine 04078
telephone: (207) 865-6112

Gaila writes, "As I was preparing to steam my lobsters one morning, a young man from Sweden yelled, 'Oh! No! They'll scream!' He was told by his father that lobsters make loud screams when they are cooking. I proved to him this wasn't the case. Also he was surprised the lobsters didn't come out of the sea already red."

To save time, Gaila uses the electric blender for making omelets and pancake batter. She likes to garnish the plates with "anything that is in season and grown in our own gardens—cherry tomatoes, zucchini slices, fresh mint and small flowers, or the leaves and small blossoms of wild strawberry plants."

Muffins ("I always have some stored in the freezer to reheat."), fruits and coffee make breakfast-to-go for early rising guests.

SHRIMP AND BRIE SCRAMBLED EGGS   Serves 10

25 eggs
2 1/2 cups nonfat milk
5 1" square pieces of brie
dash salt, pepper, and cayenne pepper
5 teaspoons chopped chives
5 teaspoons butter
2 to 3 cups frozen baby shrimp, thawed

　　This recipe is for 10 people or 5 couples. It can be prepared in 5 separate bowls as follows: Mix 5 eggs and 1/2 cup nonfat milk into each bowl. Cut the squares of brie into small pieces and add to the eggs and milk. Mix in the seasonings and 1 teaspoon chives. Heat 1 teaspoon butter in an 8" fry pan on medium heat. Pour the egg and brie mixture into the pan and add about 1/2 cup of the baby shrimp. Stir until well cooked and fluffy.

The Cain House
Chris and Marachal Gohlich
11 Main Street
Bridgeport, CA 93517
telephone: (619) 932-7040

FARMER'S BREAKFAST

Serves 6

12 eggs, beaten
4 precooked medium potatoes
1 large onion
12 slices of bacon

Peel and slice the potatoes and saute briefly in oil until brown. Slice and saute the onion. Cook the bacon until crisp.

Layer the onions and potatoes in a skillet. Add salt and pepper to taste. Pour the beaten eggs over the potatoes and cook until set. Do not overcook the eggs. Crumble the bacon and sprinkle it over the eggs. Serve at once in the skillet.

The Inn at Manchester
Stan and Harriet Rosenberg
Rt 7A, Box 41
Manchester, VT 05254
telephone: (802) 362-1793

To save preparation time for any dish made with potatoes, the Rosenbergs pre-boil the potatoes the night before. The bacon or sausage is laid out on trays and refrigerated, so it is ready to cook in the morning. For the above dish, one recipe is cooked in an iron skillet and the pan is brought to the table and placed on mats. Another recipe can be prepared and ready for the next wave of guests. "We can prepare this for up to six folks at a time. We have twenty rooms and forty people can come in at one time, so we try to find menus to suit a crowd."

For early breakfasts, the coffee pot is set up and guests may make their own coffee. Granola and other cereals plus muffins or quick breads are arranged on a tray in the kitchen.

"Our cat is a special part of our family," the Rosenberg's share, "but we generally keep her out of the kitchen and dining room during meals. A guest let her indoors one day during breakfast and Kitty headed straight for the dining room to proudly display the dead mouse she had caught!"

This dish was judged to be very good, easy, and filling. It's a dish most guests would like a lot. Grated cheese could be put on the top to vary this recipe.

FEATHERBED EGGS

Serves 4 to 6

6 slices buttered bread
salt and pepper
1 1/2 cups grated mild Cheddar cheese
1 1/2 cups milk
6 eggs

    Arrange the bread in a 9" X 13" buttered baking dish. Salt and pepper lightly and sprinkle the cheese on top. Combine the milk and eggs. Pour the milk and eggs over the bread and cheese. Cover and refrigerate overnight. In the morning, put the pan in a cold oven. Bake at 350 degrees for about one hour or until puffed and golden. Serve immediately.

*   Ellen uses lots of parsley and always has kiwi on hand. "The begonias we grow for decoration make a lovely garnish!"*

*   The judges thought that crumbled bacon could be added, if desired, to this dish. Baking time may vary.*

ELLEN'S BREAKFAST CASSEROLE

Serves 8

8 slices bread cut into cubes
1 1/2 cups shredded Cheddar cheese
10 eggs
2 cups milk
2 teaspoons dry mustard
2 teaspoons dill (optional)
brown and serve sausage or crumbled bacon
1/2 cup white wine

    Spray or butter a 9" X 13" glass baking dish and spread the bread cubes evenly to cover the bottom of the pan. Sprinkle the cheese over the bread. Beat the eggs, milk, dry mustard, and dill. Pour the egg mixture over the bread and cheese. Dot the top with cut up sausage or crumbled bacon. Drizzle white wine over the top. Cover and refrigerate overnight.
    In the morning, bake, uncovered, at 350 degrees for 50 minutes or until set.

Blushing Rose Bed and Breakfast
Ellen and Bucky Laufersweiler
11 William Street
Hammondsport, NY 14840
telephone: (607) 569-3402

*   "The taste is pleasant and the casserole is filling," said a judge. Since no amount is given for the bacon, the test recipe used four slices. The amount of wine used may vary according to taste.*

RANCHERS' EGGS

Serves 8 to 12

1 tablespoon olive oil
2 garlic cloves, crushed
2 medium onions, finely chopped
6 large tomatoes, peeled, seeded and chopped
2 ounces canned pimentos, chopped
1 green pepper, seeded and finely chopped
1 teaspoon sugar
1 teaspoon salt
1/2 teaspoon black pepper
1/2 teaspoon coriander
12 eggs
1 1/2 cups grated Cheddar cheese
1 tablespoon butter, cut into small pieces
1/4 teaspoon chili powder

Preheat the oven to 450 degrees. In a large frying pan heat the oil over medium heat. Add the garlic and onions and stir occasionally for 5 to 7 minutes or until they are soft and translucent, but not brown. Add the tomatoes, pimentos, green pepper, sugar, salt, pepper, and coriander. Reduce the heat to low and simmer, stirring frequently. Cook about 15 to 20 minutes.

Spoon the tomato mixture into a large buttered baking dish. With the back of a tablespoon, make 12 hollows in the mixture. Place one egg in each hollow. Sprinkle the cheese over the eggs. Dot butter over the cheese and sprinkle with chili powder.

Bake the eggs for 6 to 8 minutes or until the cheese is golden brown and the eggs have set. Serve immediately with crusty French bread and butter.

Chestnut Charm Bed and Breakfast
Barbara Stensvad
1409 Chestnut Street
Atlantic, Iowa 50022
telephone: (712) 243-5652

A judge's comment, "This dish is very delicious. It is different, with lots of vegetables. It would be good with fresh, garden tomatoes. The eggs may take longer to bake than indicated in the recipe."

BAKED DEVILED EGGS

Serves 4 to 6

6 hard boiled eggs
3 tablespoons sour cream
1 teaspoon prepared mustard
1/4 teaspoon salt
1/4 teaspoon pepper
1 tablespoon butter
1/2 cup chopped red and green pepper
1/3 cup chopped onion
1 can cream of mushroom soup
1 cup sour cream
1/2 cup shredded cheddar cheese

Cut the eggs lengthwise. Remove the yolks and set aside the whites. Blend into the mashed yolks 3 tablespoons sour cream, mustard, salt, and pepper. Fill the whites with the mixture.

In a large skillet, melt the butter and saute the pepper and onion until tender. Remove from heat. Stir in the soup and sour cream.

Place half the soup mixture in a casserole dish. Add the eggs, cut side up, in a single layer. Pour the remaining soup mixture over top. Sprinkle with cheese.

At this point the casserole may be covered with plastic wrap and refrigerated overnight.

Bake at 350 degrees for 20 minutes or until the cheese is melted. Allow to stand for 5 minutes before serving.

Farm Fortune Bed and Breakfast
Chad and Phyllis Combs
204 Linekiln Road
New Cumberland, PA 17070
telephone: (717) 774-2683

"We served this on toasted English muffins," commented one of the judges. "It was delicious! We would fix this again for company. It took twenty minutes to half an hour to prepare once the eggs were hard cooked and was easy to make the night before."

EGGS HERSEY

Serves 8

8 hard cooked eggs
1/3 cup butter melted
1 1/2 teaspoons Worcestershire sauce
mustard to taste
4 slices boiled ham, ground
several sprigs of fresh parsley, chopped
4-5 green onions with tops, chopped
3 cups rich white sauce
1 to 1 1/2 cups grated Parmesan or mild Cheddar cheese

Cut the eggs lengthwise and lift out the yolks. Mash the yolks. Add the melted butter, Worcestershire sauce, and mustard. Add the ground ham, parsley, and onions. Stuff the mixture into the whites. Place eggs, cut side up, in a greased baking dish or individual ramekins. Top with white sauce.

This may be made ahead and refrigerated at this point.

Bake in a 350 degree oven for 15 to 20 minutes. Top with grated cheese halfway through baking.

Hersey House
Gail Orell and Lynn Savage
451 N. Main Street
Ashland, OR 97520
telephone: (503) 482-4563

This is very good served with graham bread. See Quick Breads for the recipe.

FRESH VEGETABLE FRITTATA

Serves 4 to 6

6 eggs
1/2 teaspoon salt
1/2 teaspoon pepper
3 tablespoons butter
3 small zucchini, sliced
1 large onion, sliced
1 clove garlic, minced
1 cup fresh mushrooms, sliced
2 cups fresh spinach, washed and cut into 1" strips
1 teaspoon Italian herb seasoning
1 tablespoon chopped parsley
1 cup grated Parmesan or Swiss cheese
3 tablespoons butter

Beat the eggs in a large bowl and add salt and pepper. Melt 3 tablespoons butter in a large oven proof skillet (an iron skillet works well) over medium heat. Saute the zucchini, onion, garlic, and mushrooms until limp. Add the spinach and toss until wilted. Sprinkle with parsley and Italian seasoning. Remove from heat.

Stir about 3/4 cup cheese into the eggs. Add the cooked vegetable mixture to the egg and cheese mixture and blend. Wipe the skillet. Then add the remaining 3 tablespoons butter to the skillet. Place over medium heat. When the butter begins to foam, add the egg and vegetable mixture and turn the heat to low. Cook the eggs without stirring until they are set and thickened.

Preheat the broiler. When only the top of the eggs is still moist, sprinkle the remaining cheese over the eggs and place the skillet under the broiler until the top is a light golden brown. Go around the edges of the skillet with a sharp knife to loosen the frittata. Slide the loosened frittata onto a warm plate. Cut it into wedges and serve.

Five Gables Inn
Paul and Ellen Morissette
Murray Hill Road
East Boothbay, ME 04544
telephone: (207) 633-4551

Paul and Ellen have found that writing the menus in advance helps save time grocery shopping and planning breakfasts. They set up the dining room the night before to avoid an early morning rush.

Fresh Vegetable Frittata was judged to be "nutritious, different, and delicious!" A cooking hint was to be sure to use a large skillet.

GARDEN VEGETABLE STRATA   Serves 8

8 slices of bread, cubed
1 pound sausage, ham, or bacon (optional)
2 tablespoons chopped onion
3 tablespoons chopped green pepper
1 cup chopped, precooked broccoli
12 eggs
1 cup hot water
1 cup milk
2 tablespoons chicken bouillon
1/4 teaspoon pepper
1/2 teaspoon onion powder
1 tablespoon parsley
2 cans cream of chicken soup
4 sliced, red tomatoes
2 cups shredded Cheddar cheese

Butter a 9" X 13" baking dish and cover the bottom with the cubed bread. Layer the meat, onion, green pepper, and broccoli. Mix the eggs, water, milk, chicken bouillon, seasonings, and soup. Pour the egg mixture over the ingredients in the baking dish. Sprinkle the cheese over the top and layer the sliced tomatoes on top of the cheese. Cover and refrigerate overnight. In the morning, bake at 325 for 35 minutes or until set. Baking time will vary. Cool 15 minutes before serving.

This can be made vegetarian style without meat.

> Rancho San Gregorio
> Bud and Lee Raynor
> 5086 La Honda Road
> Rt. 1 Box 54
> San Gregorio, CA 94074

The judges thought that this would also make a good brunch or light supper dish.

HAM AND POTATO PIE SUPREME   Serves 8

2 tablespoons oil
1/3 cup chopped green pepper
1/2 cup chopped onions
1/8 teaspoon ground pepper
8 slices lean ham, cooked and drained
2 cups hash brown potatoes
1/2 cup grated Parmesan cheese
6 eggs
1/2 cup cottage cheese
8 ounce can mushrooms, drained
creole or picante sauce (optional)

    In a small skillet, saute the onions and green peppers in the oil for 5 minutes or until tender. Stir in the ground pepper. Set the mixture aside. Line a 9" X 13" sprayed baking pan with the ham slices. Top the ham with a 1/2 inch layer of hash brown potatoes. Add a layer of Parmesan cheese. Beat the eggs with the cottage cheese until smooth. Add the mushrooms, green peppers, and onions and pour this mixture over the cheese layer. Bake at 325 degrees for 40 to 45 minutes or until set. Serve with creole or picante sauce, if desired.

Cameron's Crag
Kay and Glen Cameron
P.O. Box 526
Pt. Lookout, MO 65726
telephone: (800) 695-1546

*   This dish is from a cookbook written by Kay Cameron called "Breakfasts Ozark Style." She includes a tip for when a casserole isn't ready and the appetites are. "Spray a plate with vegetable coating spray, place a few blobs of casserole on it, and then zap in the microwave on low for a few minutes until set. Continue baking the rest of the casserole while you eat the appetizer."*

*   This was judged an excellent casserole. It was hearty, but not heavy. When this recipe was kitchen tested, we used three cups of hash browned potatoes.*

WESTWAY'S SOUTHWESTERN SOUFFLE Serves 8

2 cups shredded Monterey Jack cheese
2 cups shredded medium sharp cheese
3 4 ounce cans whole green chilies
6 eggs
1 cup flour
4 cups whole milk
salt and pepper to taste

Butter the bottom of a 3 quart souffle dish. Cut chilies into 1" pieces. Layer the cheeses and chilies in the bottom of the dish. Beat together the eggs, flour, milk, salt, and pepper. Pour the egg mixture over the cheeses. This should fill about half of the dish. Bake in a preheated 350 degree oven for 1 hour. Let it stand 5 minutes before serving. Serve with homemade guacamole, sour cream, homemade salsa, and warm fresh corn or flour tortillas.

This recipe was from our Hispanic housekeeper's grandmother, a native of the Southwest.

> Westways "Private" Resort Inn
> Darrell Trapp
> P. O. Box 41624
> Phoenix, Arizona 85080
> telephone: (602) 582-3868

For extra early risers, Darrell Trapp says, "We offer a deluxe continental breakfast tray with a pre-selected menu which consists of fresh squeezed juice, homemade pastry of the day, cold cereal or homemade granola, cold boiled (hard cooked) eggs colored like Easter eggs, and coffee, tea, or herbal tea. We deliver the tray to the room at the determined time. The guests can choose to eat in their room, on the patio-courtyard, pool side, or at the kitchen counter." Trapp types colorful, inexpensive labels which list the guests' names and room numbers, and the requested breakfast times to put on each continental breakfast tray.

A judge's comment: "This was good and easy to prepare. It would also be good for brunch or dinner."

TOSTADA QUICHE DEL REY

Serves 6

1 9" pie crust
1 1/2 cups shredded Cheddar cheese (6 ounces)
8 ounces ground beef
1/4 cup chopped onion
1 (4 ounce) can chopped green chilies
1 or 2 tablespoons taco seasoning mix
3 eggs
pepper to taste
1 1/2 cups half and half

Serve With:
2 avocados, peeled, seeded and mashed
1 garlic clove, minced
3 tablespoons lemon juice
2 tomatoes, chopped
medium salsa
sour cream
shredded lettuce
corn and flour tortillas
1 medium can refried beans

The night before, prepare one 9" pie crust. Preheat the oven to 400 degrees. Bake the pie crust for 15 minutes. Remove it from the oven and set it aside. In a medium skillet, combine beef, onion, chilies less 1 tablespoon, and taco seasoning mix. Cook over medium high heat, stirring occasionally, until the beef is browned and the onion is tender. Drain the beef mixture. Layer the Cheddar cheese and beef mixture in the pastry shell. Refrigerate the filled pastry shell until morning.

The next morning, preheat oven to 375 degrees. In a medium bowl, combine the eggs, half and half, and pepper. Beat with a fork or whisk until mixed well. Pour the egg mixture over the ground beef mixture in the crust. Bake 45 minutes or until a knife inserted off-center comes out clean. Let stand 10 minutes before serving.

In a small bowl, mix avocados, garlic, and lemon juice. Stir in 1 chopped tomato and 1 tablespoon green chilies. Refrigerate until ready to serve. This side dish could be prepared ahead.

To serve, cut the quiche into six pieces and garnish with shredded lettuce and cheese. Serve side dishes of shredded lettuce, 1 chopped tomato, the avocado mixture, warmed refried beans, salsa, and sour cream. Warm tortillas between layers of damp paper towels in the microwave and roll or fold to serve.

The King's Cottage, A Bed and Breakfast Inn
Karen and Jim Owens
1049 East King Street
Lancaster, PA 17602
telephone: (717) 397-1017

Judge's comment: "Wow! We'll have this again."

STUFFED TUNA BREAD   Serves 8

1 loaf French bread
8 ounces softened cream cheese
1/2 cup chopped celery
1/4 cup snipped parsley
1/3 cup chili sauce
2 tablespoons chopped onion
2 teaspoons lemon juice
1 can drained tuna
2 chopped hard cooked eggs
2 tablespoons sliced pimento

With a serrated knife, trim off one inch from each end of the bread and discard. Cut the loaf in half horizontally. Hollow out each half, leaving a 1/2 inch border. Reserve the bread crumbs and set them aside. In a medium bowl, combine the cream cheese, celery, parsley, chili sauce, onion, and lemon juice. Stir in the tuna, egg, pimento, and finely crumbled reserved bread. Mix well. Spoon the tuna mixture into the bread halves and reassemble the bread. Wrap and refrigerate the loaf for two hours or overnight. To serve, cut the loaf into 1 1/2" slices.

Scotland Bridge Inn
Duke and Sylvia S. B. Jansen
One Scotland Bridge Road
York, ME 03909
telephone: (207) 363-4432

This made a delicious, fancy sandwich, in the judge's opinion. She reports that everyone who tried it really liked it and recommends this for a later morning breakfast or brunch.

D B'S HOT CHICKEN SALAD   Serves 5

2 1/2 cups cooked chicken
2 hard boiled eggs, diced
1 cup cooked rice
1/2 teaspoon salt
1 tablespoon lemon juice
3/4 cup celery, diced
1/2 small onion, diced
1/2 cup mayonnaise
1 can mushroom soup
1/2 to 3/4 cup slivered almonds
1 small can of mushrooms, drained (optional)
bread crumbs

Cut the chicken into bite sized chunks. Mix all the ingredients together well and put into a 9" X 13" casserole. Top with bread crumbs. Cover with plastic wrap and refrigerate overnight.

In the morning, bake at 350 degrees for 40 to 45 minutes.

Sugarbush Bed and Breakfast
William and Maryann Mahanna
RR 1 Box 227 Old Poland Road
Barneveld, NY 13304
telephone: ((315) 896-6860

The Mahannas have found that the best way to be prepared for breakfast guests is, "to start the day or night before." Maryann washes all the fruits and garnishes ahead and stores them separately in plastic bags in the refrigerator. She broils the bacon and refrigerates it in a plastic container. She also sets the table in the evening.

Some garnishes are meant to be eaten. For instance, when Maryann prepares a platter of scrambled eggs and bacon, she garnishes it with slices of tomato and grated cheese. Then she sprinkles minced parsley over the cheese and heats the entree until the cheese melts.

The judges thought that this dish had a very good flavor and texture. It is a hearty, satisfying, and unusual morning dish which would also be good for brunch or supper.

BREAKFAST FLAN   Serves 8

1/2 cup sugar
7 eggs
1 8 ounce can evaporated milk
1 can sweetened condensed milk
1/8 teaspoon salt
1 teaspoon vanilla
1/2 cup brandy (optional)
2 cups hot milk (can be low fat)
orange peel

Melt the sugar in a small pan over medium heat, stirring constantly. Pour the melted sugar into a 2 quart pyrex dish and swirl the sugar to cover the bottom of the dish. Set aside. In a bowl, whisk the eggs, add the canned milks, salt, vanilla, and brandy. Heat the regular milk in a sauce pan with a strip of orange peel. Add the hot milk to the egg mixture and pour it into the prepared glass baking dish. Cover and place the flan dish in a pan of boiling water. The water should come half way up the side of the pyrex dish. Bake at 325 degrees for 45 minutes. The flan is done when a knife inserted in the center comes out clean. Remove the flan dish from the pan of water and refrigerate.

Presentation: Loosen the sides of the flan with a spatula. Unmold the flan onto a large plate with sides. Cut it into 8 wedges. Serve each wedge topped with blackberry or raspberry puree. Serve with hot breads and fresh fruit. This also makes an excellent dessert, sliced into 16 wedges.

The Inn on South Street
Jacques and Eva Downs
P.O. Box 478 A South Street
Kennebunkport, Maine 04046
telephone: (207) 967-5151

The Downs share some ideas to make their breakfasts attractive. Eva writes, "I like to use stemware, good china, and silver. The plates are garnished with leaves and flowers or berries. I "plate up" the breakfast, so the first impression is a whole."

They make a tray for early risers with a variety of breads, jam, and butter. If the breads are wrapped in plastic wrap, they can be prepared the evening before and left in the guests' room. An insulated urn of coffee or tea is also ready for the guests.

The judges thought this dish was very good. It had a rich flavor. The fruit puree makes an excellent topping.

KAISERSCHMARRN

Serves 10

10 large eggs
2 cups unbleached whole wheat flour
2 cups milk
2/3 cup confectioners sugar
2 teaspoons salt
2 cups raisins
2/3 cup fine sugar
dash of cold water

Topping:
1 cup confectioner's sugar
raspberry syrup

Separate the eggs. Combine the egg yolks, flour, milk, confectioner's sugar, salt, and raisins. Mix well. Beat the whites with the fine sugar and a dash of cold water until very firm. Gently fold the egg white mixture into the flour mixture and pour it into a very large frying pan that has been greased and preheated. When the bottom of the mixture is browned, place the pan under the broiler until the top is golden brown. Tear the Kaiserschmarrn into little pieces with two forks. Divide it into individual dishes. Sprinkle each serving with confectioner's sugar and serve with syrup.

The Lyon and the Lambe Inn
Henri and Barbara Brod
988 Lawrence at Tenth
Eugene, Oregon 97401
telephone: (503) 683-3160

Henri and Barbara suggest some interesting ways that they present their breakfast dishes. When they are serving a crowd, they choose a one dish entree and garnish each plate with cantaloupe and honeydew slices, strawberries and kiwi slices. This saves time, dishes, and also looks pretty. "We have just begun to use nasturtiums for garnish. They are great with fluffy scrambled eggs." For an attractive garnish, strawberries can be hulled and the hull replaced with a sprig of mint. For the above Kaiserschmarrn, the Brods suggest, "When strawberries are at their sweetest, we slice each perfect berry in half and surround the plate of Kaiserschmann in a continuous ring and then add dollops of whipped cream every two or three inches."

Guests who wish to have breakfast "at the crack of dawn" are served coffee or tea, a hot muffin or croissant, and juice. The Brods believe that every guest deserves their attention.

The judge commented that this dish looks interesting and is different from the usual breakfast fare. It would be liked very much by guests.

PLUM CHEESE BLINTZES

Serves 4

Crepes:

4 eggs
4 tablespoons butter, melted
2 2/3 cups milk
2 cups flour
1 teaspoon salt

Cheese Filling:

2 cups cottage cheese, strained
1 egg
2 tablespoons powdered sugar
1/2 teaspoon vanilla
1/4 teaspoon cinnamon
1 cup sour cream

Plum Sauce:

1/4 cup butter
1/2 cup sugar
2 teaspoons cornstarch
1/8 teaspoon nutmeg
4 cups fresh plums, quartered and pitted
1/2 teaspoon vanilla
juice and grated peel of one small orange

To make crepes: Blend all crepe ingredients in a blender. Pour 1/4 cup batter per crepe into a non-stick crepe pan. Turn in a few seconds when the top forms beads of moisture. Cook briefly on the second side. Set the crepes aside.

To make plum sauce: Melt butter in a large pot. Stir in sugar, cornstarch, and nutmeg. Mix in plums, turning to coat with sugar. Stir occasionally over medium heat for 3-5 minutes until juice forms a thick sauce. Remove from heat. Stir in vanilla, orange juice and grated peel. Return to heat and stir 2-3 minutes until sauce boils and thickens slightly. Strain sauce.

To make cheese filling: Blend all filling ingredients.

To assemble blintzes: Put up to 2 tablespoons Cheese Filling in the center of each crepe. Fold in the two sides, then the two ends, so the blintz is square.

Place 3 tablespoons strained sauce on the bottom of an oven proof plate. Add two blintzes and top with 1/3 cup sauce. Bake in a preheated oven at 350 degrees for 20 minutes.

Hersey House
Gail Orell and Lynn Savage
451 N. Main Street
Ashland, OR 97520
telephone: (503) 482-4563

GERMAN PANCAKE

Serves 8

9 eggs
1 1/2 cup milk
1 cup flour
1/4 teaspoon salt
1 teaspoon almond extract
1 teaspoon lemon rind

Preheat the oven to 425 degrees. Generously butter 8 individual 4" to 5" dishes. Whisk together the above ingredients. Divide the batter among the 8 individual preheated and buttered dishes. Bake at 425 degrees for 20 minutes. Reduce the heat to 350 degrees and bake for 10 minutes.

Presentation: Sprinkle with powdered sugar. Remove the pancakes from the baking dishes to individual plates. Fill the centers with fresh fruits like peaches or berries or spiced cooked apples. Garnish the plates with melon slices and serve. Vanilla flavored yogurt is very good with this.

Apple Filling:
10 apples, peeled, cored, and sliced
1 cup raisins
1/2 teaspoon cinnamon
1/4 teaspoon cloves
1/4 teaspoon nutmeg
1/3 cup brown sugar

Place the apple slices in a covered dish and microwave for 5 minutes on high. Stir. Cook another 5 minutes. Add the raisins, spices, and brown sugar. Stir and serve.

> The Inn on South Street
> Jacques and Eva Downs
> P. O. Box 478 A South Street
> Kennebunkport, Maine 04046
> telephone: (207) 967-5151

The judge said this dish looked good and tasted great. The whole family really liked it.

BEST EVER GRANOLA

Makes about 22 cups

12 cups regular oats
2 cups wheat germ
1 cup oat bran
1 cup sunflower seeds
1 cup sesame seeds
3/4 cup brown sugar
1 teaspoon salt
3/4 cup oil
2/3 cup water
2/3 cup honey
1 tablespoon vanilla
1 cup raisins
1 1/2 cups coconut (optional)
2 cups nuts (optional)

Mix all the dry ingredients, except the raisins, in a large bowl. Add the oil, water, honey, and vanilla to the dry ingredients and mix well. Place on a large, lightly oiled rectangular cake pan. Bake at 325 degrees for 1 hour 15 minutes, stirring occasionally to prevent burning. Add the raisins after removing the granola from oven. Cool and store in an airtight container.

> Mt. Ashland Inn
> Elaine and Jerry Shanafelt
> 550 Mt. Ashland Road
> Ashland, Oregon 97520
> telephone: (503) 482-8707

At Mt. Ashland Inn, the Shanafelts report the most harried kitchen moments, "seem to deal with making coffee. We have made coffee with whole beans which we have forgotten to grind or without any coffee at all! We have also forgotten to put the coffee carafe under the spout and coffee has spilled out all over the counter." One morning the pancake batter kept sticking to the griddle. Luckily, Elaine and Jerry had a prepare ahead French toast in the freezer. They quickly switched to a new entree without the guests being aware of the problem.

"We accompany all entrees with various fruit garnishes and sprays of herbs or greens to compliment the entree and add color. Sometimes the fruits lend themselves to making pictures, such as a falling star made with a slice of star fruit and a melon slice, or butterflies made with pineapple wedges, parsley, and grapes."

One judge's eighth grade daughter took samples of several varieties of granola to school to have her friends "judge" them during lunch. The assistant principal saw the commotion and moved in for a closer look. He ended up being a granola taster, too. The middle school opinion is that homemade granola is pretty tasty stuff.

BREAKFAST GRANOLA

Makes about 8 cups

4 cups old fashioned oatmeal
1 cup dry nonfat milk
1 cup wheat germ
1/2 cup chopped almonds or peanuts
1 tablespoon cinnamon
1 1/4 cups packed brown sugar
1/4 cup water
3/4 cup oil
2 teaspoons vanilla
1/2 cup raisins (added later)

Combine the first 5 ingredients. Mix the sugar, oil, warm water, and vanilla in a small bowl. Pour the sugar mixture over oat mixture and stir until well combined. Spread the granola on a large cookie sheet and bake at 200 degrees for two hours or until dry, stirring every half hour, for two hours or until dry. Cool and mix in the raisins if desired. Store in a tightly covered container.

Blushing Rose Bed and Breakfast
Ellen and Bucky Laufersweiler
11 William Street
Hammondsport, NY 14840
telephone: (607) 569-3402

HONEY GRANOLA

Makes 8 to 9 cups

4 cups uncooked old fashioned oatmeal
1 1/2 cups wheat germ
1 cup grated coconut
1/4 cup powdered milk
1 1/2 teaspoons cinnamon
1 tablespoon brown sugar
1/3 cup vegetable oil
1/2 cup honey
1 tablespoon vanilla
1/2 cup sesame seeds (optional)
1/2 cup chopped nuts
1/2 cup raisins
1/2 cup chopped dried fruit

Mix the dry ingredients in a large bowl. Combine the oil, honey, and vanilla in a small bowl and warm the mixture in the microwave. Add the oil mixture to oatmeal mixture and combine well. Spread the granola on a greased cookie sheet. Bake at 200 degrees for two hours, stirring every half hour. (Or bake at 250 degrees for one hour or 300 degrees for 30 minutes.) When toasted, add the raisins, nuts, and dried fruit.

> Blushing Rose Bed and Breakfast
> Ellen and Bucky Laufersweiler
> 11 William Street
> Hammondsport, NY 14840
> telephone: (607) 569-3402

The judges found that this granola is very satisfying. It is sweet enough, with a soft, chewy crunch. The chopped dried fruit, particularly dried apricots, makes this granola exceptional.

Fruit Dishes

VIRGINIA APPLE PUFF

Serves 4

FRUITS BLUE RIBBON BREAKFAST WINNER!!

1 cup flour
1 cup milk
4 eggs
nutmeg
4 fresh apples, peeled and chopped
raisins (optional)
walnuts (optional)

Slightly beat the eggs, and add the milk and flour. Whisk to mix the ingredients. The batter will be a little lumpy. Add a hearty dash of nutmeg and set aside. In another bowl, chop the apples, add cinnamon and sugar to taste. Add the raisins and walnuts, if desired.

Preheat the oven to 400 degrees. Put a pat of butter in each of four individual small ovenproof dishes. Place the dishes in the preheated oven until the butter has melted and the dishes are hot. Remove the dishes from the oven and immediately ladle 1/2 cup batter into each dish. Top each dish with one fourth of the apple mixture and return the dishes to the oven to bake for 15 to 20 minutes until they are puffy and browned. Top with powdered sugar and serve with real maple syrup.

The Manor at Taylor's Store
Lee and Mary Lynn Tucker
Rt. 1 Box 533
Smith Mountain Lake, Virginia 24184
telephone: (703) 721-3951

Mary Lynn says, "All our dishes are offered creatively and attractively garnished. We use lots of fresh fruits, fresh herbs and edible flowers. Several of our breakfast specialties are served in individual ramekins and au gratin dishes for that individually prepared look."

Early risers find a plate of fresh fruit, fresh juice, and an assortment of homemade muffins in the refrigerator with a special note. They can make their own coffee or tea in the guest kitchen.

HONEY MINTED GRAPES

Serves 6

1 1/2 cups red seedless grapes
1 1/2 cups green seedless grapes
1/3 cup honey
1/4 cup lime juice
1 tablespoon fresh or dried mint, chopped fine

Mix all the ingredients in a large bowl. Cover and refrigerate over night. Serve with a fresh mint leaf for garnish.

Inn at Blush Hill
Pam and Gary Gosselin
Blush Hill Road
Box 1266
Waterbury, Vermont 05676
telephone: (802) 244-7529

For early risers, the Gosselins always have homemade granola or other dry cereals on hand. They make some juice and set the timer on the coffee maker for fresh brewed coffee.

RASPBERRY-BANANA TRIFLE

Serves 15

2 10 ounce boxes frozen raspberries
2 large bananas
2 large boxes instant vanilla pudding
2 pints whipping cream, whipped
2 boxes vanilla wafers

Mix the pudding as directed on the box and combine it with half the whipped cream. Drain the raspberries, saving the juice. Line the bottom and sides of a large glass bowl with vanilla wafers. Spoon in 1/3 of the pudding mixture and top with the sliced bananas. Cover with a single layer of wafers. Top with 1/3 of the pudding mixture and then the drained raspberries. Cover with another single layer of vanilla wafers, the last 1/3 of the pudding mixture, and 1/3 cup of drained raspberry juice. Top the trifle with the reserved whipped cream. Decorate the top with fresh raspberries or strawberries, if desired. Refrigerate the trifle at least 24 hours before serving.

Wedgwood Collection of Historic Inns
Carl Glassman and Nadine Silnutzer
111 West Bridge Street
New Hope, Pennsylvania 18938
telephone: (215) 862-2570

A breakfast-in-bed tray is available upon request at the inns. At the designated time, breakfast arrives complete with fresh flowers from the garden and often with a visit from Jasper, the inn dog.
Early morning breakfasts include a hearty continental breakfast tray of fruit salad, granola and yogurt, muffins, croissants, squeezed orange juice and a "good morning" note. The table has been set and the automatic coffee maker has been programmed to have fresh brewed coffee ready.

RHUBARB ROLLUPS

Serves 8

2 cups flour
2 teaspoons baking powder
1 teaspoon salt
2 tablespoons sugar
4 tablespoons shortening
1/3 cup milk
2 cups sliced rhubarb
1 cup sugar
butter

Sift the first four ingredients together. Cut in the shortening until the mixture is crumbly. Stir in the milk to make a soft dough. Knead it slightly on a floured board. Roll the dough into a rectangle 1/8" thick and spread it with the rhubarb. Sprinkle it with sugar and dot it with butter. Roll the dough up like a jelly roll. Bake the pastry, with the seam side down, on a greased cookie sheet at 350 degrees for 30 to 40 minutes until lightly browned. Slice and serve warm with cream or whipped cream.

>Lavender Inn Bed and Breakfast
>Rose Degni and Lyn Daring
>RR #1 Box 325
>Seneca Turnpike East
>Vernon, New York 13476
>telephone: (315) 829-2440

Rose and Lyn always have extra baked goods in the freezer. They also freeze quiches, souffles, and French toast casseroles for those unexpected late arrivals. They cook bacon lightly the night before and finish cooking it in the microwave in the morning. They like to serve fruit in Italian pizzelle cups made by pressing warm pizzelles over a glass.

THE COTTAGE BREAKFAST PIE

Serves 8

crust:

2 1/2 cups flour
1 teaspoon salt
1 cup shortening, chilled
1 egg yolk
enough milk to make 2/3 cup when egg yolk added

filling:

2 cups fruit
1 cup sugar
1 teaspoon cinnamon
3 tablespoons cornstarch
1 tablespoon lemon zest
1 tablespoon lemon juice
cereal (corn flakes, bran, etc.)
1 egg white

Combine the flour and salt. Cut in the chilled shortening. Beat the egg yolk and add enough milk to make 2/3 cup liquid. Slowly pour the egg yolk mixture into the flour mixture while stirring with a fork until all the flour is moistened.

Divide the dough in half and put each half into a small plastic bag and flatten. Store the dough in the refrigerator at least one hour or overnight.

To prepare the fruit, chop fruit of the season such as apples, pears, cranberries, raspberries, strawberries, or other berries. Mix the sugar, cinnamon, and cornstarch. Add this mixture to the fruit. Mix in the lemon zest and sprinkle on the lemon juice. Mix thoroughly and let the mixture set for an hour or overnight in the refrigerator.

Prepare the individual tart pans by spraying them with non-stick spray. Break off a third or a fourth of the dough in the plastic bag. Put the dough on a piece of waxed paper and sprinkle with a little flour. Using a marble rolling pin, roll out the dough very thinly and twice as big as the tart pan. Place the dough in the tart pan.

Brush the beaten egg white on the dough. Put a layer of cereal on the dough. Heap on about a cup of the drained fruit. Wrap the sides of the dough up around the fruit. Brush the dough with egg white. Put the tart in the freezer until ready to bake.

To bake, put the tart pans on a cookie sheet. Bake at 375 degrees for 40 to 50 minutes or until nicely browned and bubbly.

The Cottage
Robert and Carol Emerick
3829 Albatross Street
San Diego, California 92103
telephone: (619) 299-1564

KIWI PIZZA

Serves 8

Crust:

1 cup flour
1/4 cup powdered sugar
1/2 cup softened butter

Cut the butter into the flour and sugar. Add a few drops of water if necessary. Squeeze the dough into a ball and knead it on a floured surface until it is smooth and pliable. Roll the dough to fit a 9" or 10" pie plate or pizza pan. Bake the crust for 15 to 20 minutes at 325 degrees until it is lightly browned.

Topping:

1 cup mashed kiwi (4 or 5 kiwis)
5 tablespoons sugar
1 tablespoon plus 1 teaspoon cornstarch

Mix the mashed kiwi, sugar, and cornstarch in a saucepan. Bring the mixture to a boil, stirring constantly. Set the topping aside to cool.

Filling:

8 ounces cream cheese
1/2 cup powdered sugar
1/2 teaspoon vanilla
1/4 teaspoon lemon juice

Mix the cream cheese, powdered sugar, vanilla, and lemon juice in a small bowl. Spread the filling over the cooled crust. Spread the cooled topping over the filling. Garnish the top with sliced kiwis.

Wedgwood Collection of Historic Inns
Carl Glassman and Nadine Silnutzer
111 West Bridge Street
New Hope, Pennsylvania 18938
telephone: (215) 862-2570

GERANIUM LEAF SORBET

Serves 4 to 6

12 rose geranium leaves
6 tablespoons sugar
1 1/4 cups water
juice of 1 large lemon
1 egg white
4 to 6 tiny geranium leaves to decorate

Pick the rose geranium leaves and use them right away because the fragrance fades quickly. Wash the geranium leaves and shake them dry. Put the sugar and water in a pan and boil the mixture until the sugar has dissolved. Put the geranium leaves in the pan, cover it, and turn off the heat. Let the mixture cool for 10 minutes.

When the flavor is satisfactory, strain the syrup into a rigid container, add the lemon juice, and let it cool. Freeze the mixture until it is semi-frozen, about 45 minutes to 1 hour. Fold in the stiffly beaten egg white. Continue to freeze the sorbet until it is a firm mush, about 1 hour. Serve the sorbet in glass dishes and garnish each serving with a tiny rose geranium leaf.

The Cottage
Robert and Carol Emerick
3829 Albatross Street
San Diego, California 92103
telephone: (619) 299-1564

Carol shares a helpful tip, "I have a separate refrigerator for fruit and baking supplies. Fresh fruit is stored on trays, unwashed, until the time it is used. This saves a lot of time because I only need to shop once a week for fruit."

For early breakfasts-to-go, Carol puts "moist apple muffins" into a small, decorative bakery box with handles to make breakfast easy to carry.

PRINCELY PEACH SOUP   Serves 4

6 large, very ripe peaches
4 tablespoons sour cream
1/4 cup orange juice
1/8 cup lemon juice
1/4 cup powdered sugar
1/8 teaspoon cinnamon
nutmeg and ground cloves to taste
whipped cream and mint sprigs for garnish

   Peel, core, and dice the peaches. In a food processor or blender, puree the peaches until they are a smooth consistency. Add the sour cream, orange and lemon juices, and powdered sugar. Mix until well blended. Add the spices and mix again. Refrigerate the soup for at least 4 hours, and serve cold. Garnish with a dollop of whipped cream and a sprig of mint.

>The King's Cottage, A Bed and Breakfast Inn
>Karen and Jim Owens
>1049 East King Street
>Lancaster, Pennsylvania 17602
>telephone: (717) 397-1017

CHILLED STRAWBERRY SOUP   Serves 6

1 quart fresh strawberries
2 cups warm water
4 tablespoons sugar
2 tablespoons cornstarch
1/8 teaspoon salt
1/8 teaspoon cinnamon
2 tablespoons lime or lemon juice
1/8 teaspoon vanilla

Wash and hull the strawberries. Combine the berries and water in a blender. In a saucepan, combine the sugar, cornstarch, salt, and cinnamon. Add the blended berries and stir. Bring the mixture to a boil. Simmer the soup until it thickens. Then add the lime or lemon juice and the vanilla. Serve warm or cold. The soup may be garnished with sour cream and/or fresh mint leaves.

Inn the Meadow
Yolanda and Michael Day
1045 Shannock Road
Charlestown, Rhode Island 02813
telephone: (401) 789-1473

For an early take-along breakfast, the Days send homemade muffins, granola, and pieces of fruit.
They garnish dishes with kiwi slices and edible flowers like johnny-jump-ups and honeysuckle blossoms.

TROPICAL FRUIT SALAD

Serves 8 to 10

1 mango (blush colored)
1 papaya
1/2 medium sized pineapple
2 kiwis
1 large banana
1 tablespoon lemon juice
1/4 cup shredded coconut

    Peel the mango and papaya. Scoop the seeds from the center of the papaya and set aside. Remove the pit of the mango. Dice the papaya, mango, and pineapple and put them into a serving bowl. Peel and slice the kiwis. Place 1 1/2 of the kiwis in the serving bowl and reserve the remaining 1/2 for garnish. Peel and slice the banana into a small bowl. Sprinkle the slices with lemon juice and toss. Place the banana slices in the serving bowl. Toss the salad to mix the fruits.
    Put the papaya seeds in a colander and wash them roughly to remove the coating on the seeds. Sprinkle 2 tablespoons of the seeds over the salad. They are edible and taste like a mild pepper. Sprinkle the coconut on top of the salad and arrange the kiwi slices around the edges of the bowl. Serve the salad cool.

The King's Cottage, A Bed and Breakfast Inn
Karen and Jim Owens
1049 East King Street
Lancaster, Pennsylvania 17602
telephone: (717) 397-1017

GRAPEFRUIT IN BLACKBERRY SAUCE

Serves 6

4 large grapefruits, sectioned and drained
6 tablespoons blackberry pancake syrup

Pour 1 tablespoon blackberry syrup (homemade is best) into each bottom of 6 wine glasses. Top with the grapefruit sections, divided equally. Garnish each serving with a sprig of mint and a johnny-jump-up flower.

>Sandlake Country Inn
>Margo Underwood
>8505 Galloway Road
>Cloverdale, Oregon 97112
>telephone: (503) 965-6745

APPLE CRUNCH

Serves 6 to 8

4 cups pared, cored and sliced apples
1 cup sugar
1/8 teaspoon salt
1 teaspoon cinnamon
1 tablespoon flour
3/4 cup oatmeal
3/4 cup brown sugar
1/4 teaspoon baking soda
1/4 cup butter, melted
rich milk or whipped cream

Grease a two quart baking dish. Peel and core the apples and slice them into a large bowl. In a small bowl, combine the sugar, salt, cinnamon, and flour. Sprinkle the sugar mixture over the apples. Place the seasoned apples in the bottom of the prepared baking dish. In a bowl, combine the oatmeal, brown sugar, and baking soda. Add the melted butter and stir the ingredients until the mixture looks like crumbs. Pour the crumbs on top of the apples, patting the top evenly. Bake in a 375 degree oven for about 45 minutes. Serve with rich milk or whipped cream.

> Lewrene Farm Bed and Breakfast
> Irene and Lewis Lehman
> 9738 Downsville Pike
> Hagerstown, Maryland 21740
> telephone: (301) 582-1735

"This can be served hot or cold and is a winner every time and either way. My guests enjoy seconds on this one!" writes Irene.

Lewis and Irene's bed and breakfast is a working farm where they raise and sell lots of sweet corn. One day a family asked if the Lehmans served corn on the cob. The next morning they enjoyed fresh corn on the cob, picked from the corn patch, with the rest of the breakfast.

The judges thought this was a delicious apple dish. You may, however, want to consider using less sugar if your apples are sweet because this is a very sweet recipe.

SWEDISH APPLE PIE

Serves 8 to 10

Filling:

sliced baking apples
2 tablespoons sugar
1 teaspoon cinnamon
juice of 1/2 lemon
1/4 teaspoon nutmeg

Topping:

1/2 cup butter
1/8 teaspoon salt
1 egg
1 cup sugar (scant)
2 cups flour

Garnish:

1 1/2 cups chopped walnuts

Fill a buttered 10" pie plate with sliced baking apples and sprinkle them with the 2 tablespoons sugar, cinnamon, lemon juice, and nutmeg.

Cream the butter, salt, egg, scant cup of sugar, and flour in a mixing bowl. Spread the batter on top of the apples. Cover the top with the nuts.

Bake at 350 degrees for about one hour. Make sure the batter is done in the middle. Cool the breakfast pie slightly and cut it into wedges or spoon it into serving dishes. Serve warm with cream or whipped cream.

Wedgwood Collection of Historic Inns
Carl Glassman and Nadine Silnutzer
111 West Bridge Street
New Hope, Pennsylvania 18938
telephone: (215) 862-2570

BAKED APPLES

Serves 6

6 apples
1/2 cup water
juice of one lemon
3/4 cup sugar
1 teaspoon cinnamon

Peel, core, and slice the apples into the water and lemon juice. Mix in the sugar and cinnamon and spread in a shallow 9" X 9" baking pan. Cover the apples with foil and bake at 350 degrees about 30 to 35 minutes until the apples are soft, but not mushy. Serve warm or cold.

>Bed and Breakfast of Waterville
>Stanley and Carol Sambora
>211 White Street
>Waterville, New York 13480
>telephone: (315) 841-8295

This recipe is easy to fix and is a good everyday dish that most guests will enjoy. It was a favorite of the judges because of its simple, good taste.

OVEN FRIED APPLES

Serves 6 to 8

10 cups sliced, cored, apples with peels
1 1/2 cups sugar
1 cup butter or margarine

Spread the apples in a greased, shallow baking pan. Sprinkle the sugar over the apples. Dot with the butter. Bake uncovered at 375 degrees for 45 to 60 minutes. Do not stir. Spoon the accumulated syrup over the apples the last minutes of baking. Remove the apples from the pan with a spatula, turning the apples over onto the serving platter.

>Grandview Lodge
>Stan and Linda Arnold
>809 Valley View Circle Road
>Waynesville, North Carolina 28786
>telephone: (704) 456-5212

Bacon is easily prepared by spreading it on a large sheet pan and baking it in the oven. The bacon is crispy, but does not curl.
Oven Fried Apples is an easy, delicious side dish. The judges especially enjoyed this.

BAKED STUFFED PEARS

Serves 4

4 pears, ripe and firm
1/4 cup raisins
3 tablespoons chopped walnuts
2 1/2 tablespoons sugar
1 tablespoon lemon juice
1/4 cup water
1/4 cup light corn syrup

Peel the pears, leaving the stems on. Core the pears on the blossom or bottom end.

Combine the raisins, walnuts, sugar, and lemon juice in a small bowl and mix well. Fill the cavity of each pear, dividing the filling equally.

Place the pears upright in a deep baking dish, preferably with a cover. Mix together the water and corn syrup and pour it into the baking dish. Cover the dish with the lid (or foil) and bake in a 350 degree oven for about 1 hour and 15 minutes or until the pears are easily pierced with a fork. Serve warm or cold with some of the syrup spooned over each pear.

Farm and Fortune Bed and Breakfast
Chad and Phyllis Combs
204 Linekiln Road
New Cumberland, Pennsylvania 17070
telephone: (717) 774-2683

PEAR SURPRISE

Serves 4 to 6

1 cup applesauce
1 cup mincemeat pie filling
1 cup chopped pecans or walnuts
1 (16 ounce) can pear halves
1/2 cup cream or whipping cream

Chop the nuts into medium sized pieces. Mix the applesauce, mincemeat pie filling, and nuts in a saucepan. Heat the mixture until hot, but not boiling. This can be heated in the microwave on high for 3 to 4 minutes, if desired. Drain the pears and heat them until warm or microwave them on high for 2 minutes. Place two pear halves in each serving dish and spoon the mincemeat mixture over the tops. Serve with cream.

The Bonnynook Bed and Breakfast Inn
Bonnie and Vaughn Franks
414 West Main Street
Waxahachie, Texas 75165
telephone: (214) 937-7207

Bonnie explains the origin of Pear Surprise, which is one of her favorite dishes. "We had just opened. Vaughn thought I had gotten the fruit for breakfast and I thought he had. The next morning—no fruit! I saw that I had cream, canned pears, applesauce, mincemeat pie filling, and nuts. My mother's warning came to mind, "Don't experiment on your guests." I threw all caution to the wind and came up with the recipe. Luckily, my guests loved the dish."

MAPLE POACHED PEARS

Serves 12

6 perfect Bosc pears
1/2 cup maple syrup
1 quart water
8 ounces French vanilla yogurt
2 tablespoons sour cream
12 mint sprigs
nutmeg

Peel, halve, and core the pears. Poach them until tender in the maple syrup and water. Drain the pears. Combine the yogurt and sour cream. Make a "pool" of the yogurt-sour cream mixture in the center of each of 12 serving plates. Gently slip a pear half onto each "pool" and garnish with a mint sprig at the stem ends. Dust each serving with nutmeg.

Grunberg Haus Bed and Breakfast
Christopher Sellers and Mark Frohman
RR 2 Box 1595
Route 100 South
Waterbury, Vermont 05676
telephone: (802) 244-7726

At Grunberg Haus, the pears are served on 6" crystal plates. Guests often photograph this dish and then enjoy it.

GLAZED BANANAS

Serves 1

1 banana
1 teaspoon butter
1 tablespoon brown sugar
1/2 teaspoon cinnamon
1/2 fresh orange, peeled and diced
dash of orange rind, fresh or dried

Melt the butter, brown sugar, cinnamon, orange, and rind in a saucepan over medium heat until the sauce is blended well. Slice the banana into the hot sauce and quickly saute until the banana is heated through. Orange juice may be added a little at a time if the banana mixture is too dry. Serve immediately.

Inn at Blush Hill
Pam and Gary Gosselin
Blush Hill Road
Box 1266
Waterbury, Vermont 05676
telephone: (802) 244-7529

BANANA SPLIT SUPREME

Serves 4

8 ounce container yogurt
1/4 cup raisins
1 cup granola
2 bananas, sliced lengthwise
1/4 cup pecans
fruit slice for garnish

Combine the yogurt, raisins, and granola. Spoon 1/2 cup of the mixture on each of the banana slices. Sprinkle each serving with chopped pecans. Garnish with a fruit slice.

Cameron's Crag
Kay and Glen Cameron
P.O. Box 526
Pt. Lookout, Missouri 65726
telephone: 1-800-695-1546

WINTER WINDFALL

Serves 6

Compote:

3 cups mixed dried fruit
1/2 cup thawed cranberries
2/3 cup port wine
2/3 cup strong brewed tea
  (lemon or orange is good)
2/3 cup water
zest of 1/2 lemon
juice of 1/2 lemon

topping:

2 teaspoons compote juice (from above)
1 cup ricotta cheese
2 teaspoons honey
slivered almonds for garnish

Combine all the compote ingredients except the lemon juice and bring them slowly to a boil. Cover and simmer for 20 minutes. Remove the fruit from the heat and allow it to cool. Add the lemon juice and chill thoroughly.

Beat the topping ingredients in a small bowl. Serve the fruit compote in dishes and spoon the topping on each serving. Garnish with slivered almonds.

The Lyon and the Lambe Inn
Henri and Barbara Brod
988 Lawrence at Tenth
Eugene, Oregon 97401
telephone: (503) 683-3160

Henri and Barbara like to pick berries in season and freeze them. In the winter, they layer the thawed berries with granola and plain or vanilla yogurt, so they can share a bit of Oregon summer with their guests.

HOT FRUIT COMPOTE

Serves 12

1 (20 ounce) can pineapple chunks
1 (16 ounce) can pear halves
1 jar maraschino cherries
1 (16 ounce) can peach halves
1 (16 ounce) can apricot halves

orange sauce:

1/3 cup sugar
2 tablespoons cornstarch
1/4 teaspoon salt
1/2 cup light corn syrup
1 cup orange juice
2 tablespoons orange zest

Drain the fruit. Arrange the fruit in a 13" X 9" X 2" baking dish and place the cherries in the hollows. Set aside. To make the sauce, combine the sugar, cornstarch, salt, corn syrup, orange juice, and orange zest in a saucepan. Heat the mixture to a boil. Remove from heat and pour the sauce over the fruit. Bake at 350 degrees for 30 minutes.

Prairie View Estate
Phyllis Haugrud, Carol Moses, Janet Malakowsky, and Anne Roland
Route 2 Box 443
Pelican Rapids, Minnesota 56572
telephone: (218) 863-4454

A time saving tip is to bake your favorite baked goods ahead and freeze them. Defrost the baked goods overnight and warm them in a bun warmer with moisture to give them just baked freshness.

When this hot fruit compote was being kitchen tested, the cook could hardly wait to see what her family thought of it. One son was reluctant to try even a bite. As it turns out, he thought his mom, who is also an avid gardener, had said it was hot fruit compost! Needless to say, with a bit of vocabulary clarification, he enjoyed this fruit dish very much.

Muffins

RASPBERRY-BLUEBERRY SURPRISE MUFFINS

Makes 24 muffins

MUFFIN BLUE RIBBON BREAKFAST WINNER !!

3 1/2 cups blueberry muffin mix
3/4 cup sour cream
1/2 cup milk
1 can blueberries (from the mix)
1 cup fresh or frozen raspberries

topping:
3/4 cup oatmeal
3/4 cup flour
3/4 cup brown sugar
1/3 cup butter, softened

Mix together the muffin mix, sour cream, and milk until just blended. Gently add the blueberries and raspberries. Fill 24 lined muffin tin cups half full. Mix the ingredients for the topping and spoon 1 tablespoon onto each muffin. Fill each muffin cup with the rest of the muffin mixture. Heap on the rest of the topping. Bake at 350 degrees for 25 minutes or until done. Watch that the tops don't get too brown. Serve hot!

> Beatrice McKinney
> 37 House
> 4002 Englewood
> Yakima, Washington 98908
> telephone: (509) 965-5537

To make breakfast preparation easier, Beatrice says, "I prepare the breakfast in the same order every morning, so I don't forget anything. I also have certain areas of the kitchen for the preparation of each part of the meal. Preparation is more efficient and the guests who come into the kitchen for a cup of coffee before breakfast see a well organized and always cleaned up kitchen."

Beatrice uses Port Marion dishes. She writes that she uses purple pansies to garnish the entrees. She also uses unusual fruit like star fruit for garnishes "to get the guests noticing."

RASPBERRY BRAN MUFFINS

Makes 12 muffins

1 cup fresh or frozen raspberries
1 cup flour
1 cup wheat bran
1/4 cup sugar
3 teaspoons baking powder
1/4 teaspoon salt
1 beaten egg
1 cup milk
1/4 cup cooking oil

Partially thaw the frozen raspberries, but do not let them completely thaw. Set aside.

In a bowl, stir together the dry ingredients and make a well in the center. In a small bowl, mix together the liquid ingredients. All at once, add the liquid ingredients to the dry ingredients. Stir just until moistened. Gently stir in the raspberries. Grease the bottoms of 12 muffin cups or line with paper bake cups. Fill each cup 2/3 full.

Bake at 400 degrees for about 20 minutes or until done. Remove from the pan and cool slightly on wire racks.

Barbara and Bruce Stensuad
Chestnut Charm Bed and Breakfast
1409 Chestnut Street
Atlantic, Iowa 50022
telephone: (721) 243-5652

The judges suggested that other berries or nuts could be used in place of the raspberries for variety.

BLUEBERRY-BOOTHBAY MUFFINS   Makes 12 muffins

2 cups fresh or frozen (small Maine) blueberries
2 1/2 cups flour
1/2 cup pecans
1 teaspoon baking powder
1 teaspoon baking soda
1/8 teaspoon salt
1/8 teaspoon nutmeg
1/2 teaspoon cinnamon
1 cup light brown sugar
1 1/4 cup buttermilk
1/2 cup oil
1 large egg
2 teaspoons vanilla

Preheat the oven to 375 degrees and prepare an average sized muffin pan by spraying it with butter-flavored cooking oil spray. Mix the dry ingredients together. Mix the sugar, buttermilk, oil, egg, and vanilla together. Add the liquid ingredients gently to the dry mixture, allowing the batter to remain a little lumpy. (Too much mixing takes away the light texture of the muffins.) Fold in the blueberries carefully and divide the batter into the 12 muffin cups. Bake for 18 to 20 minutes. Remove the muffins from the pan within a few minutes to keep the outside of the muffins crisp.

Anchor Watch Bed and Breakfast
Diane Campbell
3 Eames Road
Boothbay Harbor, Maine 04538
telephone: (207) 633-2284

Diane writes, "My dad lives in the apartment part of the house which includes the kitchen where I prepare breakfast. A young lady, unable to arrive on her scheduled night due to flight delays, came the next night. Because we were full, we offered her the couch in the kitchen. She accepted, and in the morning prepared her own breakfast in her nighty while Dad showered. The trust and warmth of two strangers are what B&Bs are all about!"

Guests who want an extra early breakfast usually prefer to be alone with their coffee to think about their day. Diane Campbell sets out a plate of muffins baked the evening before and a coffee pot set on automatic. Juice, cream, and butter are in the refrigerator. "If I did it any other way, the guest might feel he was imposing," she writes.

The judges thought that these light, slightly spicy muffins with lots of blueberries were delicious.

BLUEBERRY LEMON MUFFINS   Makes 15 to 18 muffins

2 eggs
1/2 cup melted butter
1 cup sugar
1 (8 ounce) container lemon yogurt
1/2 teaspoon grated lemon rind
2 cups flour
1 teaspoon baking powder
1 cup fresh blueberries

Preheat the oven to 375 degrees. In a large bowl, beat together the eggs, melted butter, and sugar. Stir in the yogurt and lemon rind. Add the dry ingredients and stir until they are just blended. Fold in the blueberries. Spoon the batter into greased muffin tins. Bake 20 minutes or until done. Makes 15 to 18 muffins.

> The Bailiwick Inn
> Anne and Ray Smith
> 4023 Chain Bridge Road
> Fairfax, Virginia 22124
> telephone: (703) 691-2266

Anne and Ray report, "Our garnishes come from our garden. We use flowers and herbs—all plants that were here in the 1800's."

BLUEBERRY ORANGE MUFFINS

Makes about 30 muffins

1 1/2 cups sugar
9 tablespoons butter
9 tablespoons margarine
1 cup milk
1/2 cup orange juice
3 eggs
4 1/2 cups flour
6 teaspoons baking powder
1 1/2 teaspoons salt
6 teaspoons orange rind
1 1/2 cups blueberries

Cream the sugar with the butter and margarine. Add the milk, orange juice, and eggs. Combine the flour (save 1/3 cup flour to dredge the blueberries in), baking powder, salt, and orange rind. Add the flour mixture to the liquid mixture and combine well. Then stir in the dredged blueberries. Bake at 350 degrees for 30 minutes.

While the muffins are still warm, mix 2 cups powdered sugar, 1/3 cup orange juice, and 1 teaspoon vanilla and spoon over the muffins.

The Welby Inn Bed and Breakfast
Betsy Rogers-Knox and David Knox
P.O. Box 774 Ocean Avenue
Kennebunkport, Maine 04046
telephone: (207) 967-4655

The judges thought the orange flavor was "surprisingly refreshing!"

BERRY STREUSEL MUFFINS

Makes 12 muffins

1 1/2 cups flour
1/2 cup sugar
2 teaspoons baking powder
1 beaten egg
1/2 cup milk
1/2 cup butter or margarine, melted
1 cup fresh or frozen berries

Pecan Streusel Topping:

1/4 cup chopped pecans
1/4 cup brown sugar
1/4 cup flour
2 tablespoons butter or margarine, melted

Preheat the oven to 375 degrees. Grease the muffin pan. Combine the streusel ingredients and stir until the mixture looks like moist crumbs. Set aside.

In a large bowl stir together the flour, sugar, and baking powder. In a small bowl, combine the milk, butter, and egg. Stir the liquid ingredients into the dry ingredients and stir just until moistened. Fill the muffin cups 2/3 full. Add the berries into the filled muffin cups. Sprinkle the pecan streusel topping over the tops.

Bake about 20 minutes or until done. Remove from the pan. Cool slightly on wire racks.

Barbara and Bruce Stensuad
Chestnut Charm Bed and Breakfast
1409 Chestnut Street
Atlantic, Iowa 50022
telephone: (721) 243-5652

REFRIGERATED APRICOT BRAN MUFFINS

Makes 6 dozen

6 cups bran cereal
2 cups boiling water
1 cup margarine
1 3/4 cup sugar
4 eggs
1 quart buttermilk
5 cups flour
5 teaspoons baking soda
1 teaspoon salt
2 cups chopped dried apricots
2 cups chopped nuts (optional)

Pour the boiling water over the bran cereal and let cool. Cream the margarine, sugar, and eggs. Add the bran cereal and buttermilk. Sift the flour, baking soda, and salt together. Combine the liquid and dry mixtures. Add the fruit and nuts. Bake the muffins for 15 to 20 minutes at 400 degrees. Store the unused batter in an airtight container in the refrigerator for up to six weeks. Be sure to write the expiration date on the container.

Hersey House
Gail Orell and Lynn Savage
451 North Main Street
Ashland, Oregon 97520
telephone: (503) 482-4563

Gail and Lynn share an unusual kitchen experience. "To prepare syrup containers for pancakes, we fill them with boiling water for twenty minutes. One especially hectic morning, a guest knocked on the kitchen door shortly after the entrees had been served. She had poured boiling water onto her pancakes. Fortunately, she was a returning guest who was amused. In spite of the incident, she rebooked for the following year."

For garnish, Gail and Lynn sometimes make miniature baskets from lemons or limes and fill them with blueberries. One morning not only had the blueberries been eaten, as expected, but someone had also added sugar and cream to the basket.

APRICOT MUFFINS

Makes 12 muffins

1 cup chopped dried apricots
3/4 cup sugar
2 tablespoons melted butter
1 egg
2 cups flour
1 teaspoon baking powder
1/4 teaspoon soda
1/2 teaspoon salt
1/4 cup water
1/2 cup orange juice
1/2 cup chopped walnuts

Soak the chopped dried apricots in warm water for 30 minutes. Cream together the sugar, melted butter, and egg. Sift together the flour, baking powder, soda, and salt. Add the flour mixture to the creamed mixture alternately with the orange juice and water. Stir in the drained apricots and the chopped nuts. Pour the batter into greased muffin cups or pans lined with paper baking cups. Bake at 350 degrees for 15 to 20 minutes.

Inn the Meadow
Yolanda and Michael Day
1045 Shannock Road
Charlestown, Rhode Island 02813
telephone: (401) 789-1473

Yolanda confides, "I can't seem to count my coffee measurements and talk to friendly guests at the same time. I often have to pour the coffee grounds back and start over!"

To save time at the inn, French toast and three varieties of homemade muffins are made ahead and put in the freezer. They can be reheated and served as needed.

APRICOT-ALMOND POUND CAKE MUFFINS

Makes 12 muffins

1 3/4 cup flour
1/2 teaspoon salt
1/4 teaspoon baking soda
1/2 cup sugar
1/2 cup softened butter
1/2 cup sour cream
1/2 teaspoon vanilla
1/2 teaspoon almond extract
2 eggs
1 cup chopped dried apricots
1/2 cup sliced almonds (divided 1/4 cup and 1/4 cup)

Preheat the oven to 350 degrees. Prepare the muffin cups. In a small bowl, stir together the flour, salt, and baking soda. In a large bowl, beat the sugar and butter with an electric mixer until well combined. Beat in the sour cream, vanilla, and almond extract until well blended. Beat in the eggs, one at a time, until well blended. Mix in the dry ingredients until just combined. Fold in the apricots and 1/4 cup almonds. Spoon the batter into the muffin tins and sprinkle the remaining almonds on top. Bake for 20 to 25 minutes. Makes 12 muffins.

Wedgwood Collection of Historic Inns
Carl Glassman and Nadine Silnutzer
111 West Bridge Street
New Hope, Pennsylvania 18938
telephone: (215) 862-2570

Carl and Nadine admit to being harried hosts one morning when they discovered that a guest had helped himself to the fresh squeezed orange juice and muffins the night before! Another morning the electric power was out and, since they are on a well, they had NO water.

PUMPKIN PECAN MUFFINS

Makes 12 muffins

1/2 cup softened butter
3/4 cup light brown sugar
1/4 cup Vermont maple syrup
2 eggs
1 cup half and half
1 cup pumpkin puree
2 cups flour
4 teaspoons baking powder
1/2 teaspoon salt
1/2 cup pecans, chopped

Beat the butter and brown sugar well. Add the maple syrup, eggs, half and half, and pumpkin puree. Beat until fluffy and light. In a separate bowl, mix the dry ingredients well. Add the wet ingredients and mix until moistened. Fold in the chopped pecans. Do not over mix. Bake in greased muffin pans at 425 degrees for 10 minutes and at 375 for another 10 minutes. Makes 12 muffins.

Inn on the Common
Michael and Penny Schmitt
Main Street
Craftsbury Common, Vermont 05827
telephone: (802) 586-9619

You may want to add more nuts, as one judge suggested.

The Schmitts like to use seasonal fruits to garnish their breakfast dishes. Early risers are offered fruit or juice, muffins, cheese, and beverage to go.

GREEN APPLE MUFFINS

Makes 12 mega muffins or 30 standard muffins

2 cups sugar
1 1/2 cups oil
3 eggs, beaten
2 teaspoons vanilla
3 cups flour
1 teaspoon baking soda
1 teaspoon salt
3 cups grated, unpeeled, Granny Smith apples (2 large)
1 cup chopped nuts

Mix the sugar and oil. Add the beaten eggs and vanilla. In a separate bowl, mix the dry ingredients. Stir the dry ingredients into the liquid ingredients. The mixture will be thick. Fold in the grated apples and nuts. Fill greased "mega" muffin cups 3/4 full. Bake at 350 to 375 degrees for 45 to 55 minutes. Check for doneness with a toothpick.

To make regular sized muffins, fill the greased muffin cups 3/4 full and bake at 375 degrees for about 20 minutes or until done.

Snowline Bed and Breakfast
Ed and Dana Klinkhart
11101 Snowline Drive
Anchorage, Alaska 99516
telephone: (907) 346-1631

Ed and Dana wrap all their homemade muffins individually in plastic wrap. They mark each with the type of muffin and the date. Then they place the muffins in separate containers in the freezer. To serve, they remove the muffins the night before or zap each muffin in the microwave for 30 seconds. Guests can select muffins of their choice from a brightly decorated basket on the table. "We have found this to be a great time saver and the muffins are also displayed attractively and are very fresh."

One judge sent a basket of these muffins in to her husband's office. The muffins quickly disappeared with rave reviews!

BANANA MUFFINS

Makes 12 muffins

A recipe for guests who cannot have any dairy products.

6 tablespoons shortening
1/2 cup sugar
2 egg replacers
1 cup mashed ripe bananas
3 tablespoons soy milk
2 cups flour
2 teaspoons baking powder
1 teaspoon baking soda
1/2 teaspoon salt

    Cream the shortening and sugar together. Add the egg replacers, bananas, and soy milk. In a separate bowl, mix together the flour, baking powder, soda and salt. Stir the banana mixture into the flour mixture and mix until just moistened. Pour the batter into a greased muffin tin. Bake at 400 degrees for 20 to 25 minutes.
    The egg replacers and soy milk are available at a good supermarket or a health food store.

Wedgwood Collection of Historic Inns
Carl Glassman and Nadine Silnutzer
111 West Bridge Street
New Hope, Pennsylvania 18938
telephone: (215) 862-2570

BRAN MUFFINS WITH MAPLE SYRUP   Makes 12 muffins

3/4 cup maple syrup
2 eggs
2 1/2 cups crushed bran flakes
1 cup sour milk
1 cup flour
1 teaspoon baking soda
1/2 cup chopped nuts

Combine the maple syrup, eggs, and crushed bran flakes. Let the mixture stand for 5 minutes. Using a wooden spoon, beat in the sour milk. Stir in the flour and baking soda and fold in the chopped nuts. Pour the batter into greased muffin pans. Bake about 20 minutes at 400 degrees.

Sugarbush Bed and Breakfast
William and Maryann Mahanna
RR 1 Box 227 Old Poland Road
Barneveld, New York 13304
telephone: (315) 896-6860

Maryann and William like to start breakfast by serving a platter of fruit. For example, they arrange thin slices of cantaloupe with whole strawberries and sliced kiwis. Another favorite way to serve fruit is to fill ice cream dishes with melon balls and blueberries.

The judges loved this delicious, easy muffin recipe!

MIKA'S MARVELOUS MUFFINS   Makes 24 muffins

1/2 cup sugar
1/3 cup orange juice
   Combine and set aside.

1 cup sugar
1/2 cup butter
1/2 cup oil
1 1/2 cups nonfat yogurt
4 cups flour
2 teaspoons baking soda
2 teaspoons salt
2 teaspoons grated orange peel
1 cup raisins
1 cup chopped walnuts

Cream the butter, oil, and sugar. Blend in the yogurt. Combine the dry ingredients and add them to the creamed mixture. Stir just until the ingredients are combined. Stir in the grated orange peel, raisins, and nuts. The batter will be stiff. Use an ice cream scoop to put the batter into muffin paper lined muffin tins. Fill each cup completely full. Bake at 350 degrees for 15 minutes. While the muffins are warm, dip each into the sugar-orange juice mixture.

>Just-N-Trails Bed and Breakfast/Farm Vacation
>Donna and Don Justin
>Route 1 Box 274
>Sparta, Wisconsin 54656
>telephone: (608) 269-4522   1-800-488-4521

Mika Oguchi is a Japanese intern at Just-N-Trails. These muffins are her favorite to make for guests. Mika will return to her family's hotel, The Ichiriki, following her internship.

There is always something new happening at Just-N-Trails from international guests and Mika's piano concerts to cows giving birth and star gazing through the telescope.

To present private breakfasts in a special way, guests are served breakfast baskets for two in the "Granary" and the "Little House on the Prairie" cabins. Matching table cloths and napkins dress up the wicker picnic hampers. For guests who must leave extra early, muffins tied in a red and white cowboy handkerchief hobo style, single serving orange juice containers, and coffee in Just-N-Trails mugs send them on their way.

CHOCOLATE CHIP MUFFINS   Makes 12 muffins

1 1/2 cup flour
1/2 cup sugar
1/4 cup unsweetened cocoa
1 teaspoon baking soda
1/2 teaspoon salt
1 teaspoon orange juice concentrate
1/2 cup orange juice
1/3 cup water
3 tablespoons oil
1 tablespoon vinegar
1 teaspoon vanilla
1/3 cup mini chocolate chips
powdered sugar

Combine the dry ingredients in a large bowl. Combine the liquid ingredients in a small bowl. Add the liquid ingredients to the dry ingredients, stirring just until moistened. Fold in the chocolate chips. Bake in greased and floured tins or paper-lined muffin cups at 375 degrees for 12 minutes or until a toothpick comes out clean. Cool the muffins and sprinkle with powdered sugar. Makes 12 muffins.

Rancho San Gregorio
Bud and Lee Raynor
5086 La Honda Road
Rt. 1 Box 54
San Gregorio, California 94074

This no cholesterol recipe is handy to have on hand for guests who want a low cholesterol breakfast.

Quick Breads

ANN'S POPPY SEED BREAD

Serves 12

QUICK BREADS BLUE RIBBON BREAKFAST WINNER !!

4 eggs
2 cups sugar
1 1/2 cups oil
3 cups flour
1 1/2 teaspoon baking soda
1 1/2 teaspoons salt
1 large can evaporated milk
2 ounce can whole poppy seed

    In a large bowl, beat the eggs well. Add the sugar and beat well. Add the oil slowly and mix well. Sift together the flour, baking soda, and salt. Beat the flour mixture slowly into the egg mixture. Slowly beat in the evaporated milk. Add the poppy seeds and beat slowly.

    Pour the batter into a greased and floured bundt pan. Hit the pan on the counter a few times to settle any trapped air bubbles. Bake for one hour at 350 degrees. Do not turn the pan upside down, but put it on a cake rack to cool for 10 minutes. Then turn the cake out. If the cake is in the pan any longer, it may stick.

> The San Sophia
> Dianne and Gary Eschman
> 330 West Pacific Avenue
> Telluride, Colorado 81435
> telephone: (303) 728-300

"This poppy seed bread is such an outstanding product that I use it instead of rolls or bread at dinner parties."

Dianne has found that a towel placed under the coffee grinder makes clean up easier. Continuously cleaning little spills in the oven saves you from a big cleaning job. Canned juices are served at The San Sophia to save time and energy.

She writes that instead of an early breakfast, she and Gary give early risers, "a firm handshake, guide them to the front porch, fix them with a sincere stare and then say, 'Have a nice day.'"

One time when a guest had a few minutes to wait for breakfast, she asked Dianne what she should do while she waited. Dianne told her to, "Reflect on your life to date and decide to make any changes you feel might be necessary." The startled guest said she would!

LEMON POPPY SEED BREAD

Makes 4 loaves

2 1/2 cups sugar
4 sticks butter
16 eggs
8 cups flour
6 teaspoons baking powder
2 teaspoons salt
3 cups milk
1 cup poppy seeds
7 lemons, juice and zest

Cream the butter and sugar in a large mixing bowl. Add the eggs and mix well. Sift the flour, baking powder, and salt. Alternately add the flour mixture and the milk to the creamed mixture. Fold in the poppy seeds, lemon zest, and lemon juice. Pour the batter into 4 greased loaf pans and bake for approximately 1 hour at 325 degrees. Sprinkle with powdered sugar if desired.

Alexander's Inn
Carolyn Lee and Mary Jo Schneider
529 East Palace Avenue
Santa Fe, New Mexico 87501
telephone: (505) 986-1431

At Alexander's Inn, serving breakfast buffet style is easy, simple, and efficient for both hosts and guests.

For early breakfasts, guests can prepare what they would like from a buffet of coffee, muffins, cereal, fruit, and juice.

POPPY SEED BREAD

Makes 2 loaves

3 cups flour
1 1/2 teaspoons salt
1 1/2 teaspoons baking powder
3 eggs
1 1/2 cups oil
2 1/2 cups sugar
1 1/2 cups milk
1 1/2 teaspoons vanilla
1 1/2 teaspoons almond flavoring
1 1/2 teaspoons butter flavoring
1 1/2 teaspoons poppy seeds

glaze:
1/4 cup orange juice
3/4 cup sugar
1/2 teaspoon almond flavoring
1/2 teaspoon butter flavor
1/2 teaspoon vanilla

In a large bowl, mix the flour, salt, and baking powder and set it aside. In another bowl, combine the rest of the ingredients. Make a hole in the center of the flour mixture and add the egg mixture. Stir for two minutes or until well blended. Pour the batter into two well greased bread pans. Bake at 350 degrees for one hour.

Combine the glaze ingredients. While the loaves are still in the pan, prick the tops of the loaves several times with a fork. Pour the glaze over the warm loaves.

Varns Guest House
Carl and Diane Eash
205 South Main Street
Middlebury, Indiana 46540
telephone: (219) 825-9666

When they have 10 or more for breakfast, the Eashes serve buffet style. For 4 or less, guests are served at the breakfast room table. Diane's mother usually prepares three types of breakfast pastries. She likes to have everything ready early so she has plenty of time to visit with the guests. "That way I can visit and not feel hurried and frustrated."

CHOCOLATE APPLESAUCE BREAD Makes 3 loaves

3/4 cup butter
2 cups sugar
3 unbeaten eggs
25 ounces apple sauce
4 cups flour
2 1/2 teaspoons baking soda
1/2 teaspoon salt
3/4 teaspoon cinnamon
4 teaspoons cocoa
mini chocolate chips (about 3 tablespoons per loaf)

Cream the butter and sugar in a large bowl. Add the eggs and mix well. Blend in the applesauce. Sift together the dry ingredients and add them to the first mixture. Pour the batter into 3 well greased loaf pans and sprinkle the tops with mini chocolate chips. Bake at 350 degrees for 1 hour. Cool the bread in the pans on a rack. This bread stays fresh for several days. Makes 3 loaves.

The Inn on South Street
Jacques and Eva Downs
P.O. Box 478 A
South Street
Kennebunkport, Maine 04046
telephone: (207) 967-5151

One judge reports that this quick bread has become one of her favorite recipes. The chocolate applesauce bread is good warm from the oven, keeps well for several days, and freezes beautifully, so there is always something yummy for a special breakfast.

EMILY'S BANANA BREAD

Serves 6

1/2 cup butter
1 cup sugar
2 eggs
1 1/2 cups mashed bananas (about 3 large bananas)
2 tablespoons sour cream
2 cups flour
1 teaspoon baking powder
1 teaspoon salt
1/2 teaspoon baking soda
1/2 cup chopped nuts

Cream the butter and sugar. Add the eggs one at a time, stirring after each. Stir in the mashed bananas and sour cream. Mix together the flour, baking powder, salt, and baking soda. Stir the dry ingredients into the banana mixture. Add the nuts. Bake in a greased loaf pan for 45 to 55 minutes at 350 degrees. Makes one loaf.

Gail and Lynn offer some time saving tips for busy hosts. When baking, measure the dry ingredients before the wet ingredients. Then you can use the same measuring cups. Plan meals so that during any "gaps" you can prepare food for the next day. As guests check in, ask what they like to drink, find out if they have any special diets, and discuss the breakfast menu to cut down on last minute changes.

Hersey House
Gail Orell and Lynn Savage
451 North Main Street
Ashland, Oregon 97520
telephone: (503) 482-4563

GRANDMOM'S BANANA BREAD   Serves 6-8

3/4 cup sugar
1/2 cup oil
2 eggs
1 generous cup very ripe mashed bananas
1 3/4 cup flour
2 teaspoons baking powder
1/2 teaspoon baking soda
1/2 teaspoon salt

In a large bowl, combine the sugar, oil, eggs, and bananas. Mix on medium speed until well blended and a pale yellow color. In another bowl, mix all the dry ingredients until well blended. With the mixer running, incorporate the dry ingredients into the banana mixture. Mix until well blended. Pour the batter into a lightly greased loaf pan and bake in a preheated 325 degree oven for one hour or until a toothpick inserted comes out clean. Makes one loaf.

"This bread is delicious "stale" and toasted with a little bit of peanut butter, although we rarely have leftovers to enjoy this way."

This batter can also be used to make 18 muffins. The baking time is about 20 minutes.

Thomas Bond Bed and Breakfast
Gerald and Lisa Dunn
129 South 2nd Street
Philadelphia, Pennsylvania 19106
telephone: (215) 923-8523

Lisa writes, "Jerry and I are generally very organized and have everything prepared the evening before. Usually our guests come down for breakfast late and a few at a time. One recent morning we weren't so 'ready' and everyone came down all at once! Talk about a frenzied pace! But, we survived and our guests were fine."

Gerald and Lisa enjoy preparing theme breakfasts like pumpkin muffins at Halloween—with table decorations, of course. They also invite jazz ensembles to play during Sunday brunch for a fun and relaxing atmosphere.

DRIED FRUIT CREAM SCONES   Serves 12

2 cups flour
1 tablespoon baking powder
1/2 teaspoon salt
1/4 cup sugar
3/4 cup finely chopped dried fruits
   (apricots, peaches, apples)
1/2 cup golden raisins
1 1/4 cups heavy cream

Topping:
3 tablespoons butter
2 tablespoons sugar

   In a bowl, combine the flour, baking powder, salt, and 1/4 cup sugar. Stir with a fork until well mixed. Add the dried fruit and raisins. Stir in the cream and mix lightly until the dough holds together. The dough will be sticky.
   Transfer the dough to a lightly floured board and knead 8 or 9 times. Pat the dough into a 10 inch circle. Spread the melted butter over the dough and sprinkle it with 2 tablespoons sugar.
   Cut the circle into 12 wedges and place each wedge on a greased baking sheet, allowing one inch between each piece. Bake at 400 degrees for about 12 minutes or until the scones are light brown on the bottom.

Locust Lane Farm Bed and Breakfast
Ruth and Don Shoup
5590 Kessler Cowlesville Road
West Milton, Ohio 45383
telephone: (513) 698-4743

Nasturtium blossoms and parsley make an attractive garnish on serving plates. The Shoups also use mint sprigs on servings of fresh fruit. Ruth has learned that ANYTHING she can do the night before makes breakfast easier.

The judges thought that these scones were very tasty and an interesting kind of bread for breakfast. The dried fruit made these special. The scones were great with butter and jam!

BERRY COBBLER

Serves 12

1 cup flour
1 cup sugar
4 teaspoons baking powder
1 teaspoon salt
1 cup half and half
1 teaspoon vanilla

Mix the above ingredients together and pour into a greased 9" X 13" pan.

3 cups fresh berries
3/4 cup sugar
1 stick butter
1 teaspoon cinnamon

Mix the berries with the sugar and pour the mixture over the batter. Do not stir the berries and batter together. Cut the butter into little pieces and dot the top. Sprinkle with the cinnamon. Bake 45 to 60 minutes. Serve with whipped cream or ice cream.

Some berry suggestions:
   blueberries
   blackberries
   cherries
   raspberries
   strawberries

Wedgewood Collection of Historic Inns
Carl Glassman and Nadine Silnutzer
111 West Bridge Street
New Hope, Pennsylvania 18938
telephone: (215) 862-2570

Carl and Nadine repeat experienced innkeepers' sage advice, "Prepare as much as possible the day before!!" It also helps to organize the kitchen "for a smooth breakfast flow."

WESTERN COWBOY BAKING POWDER BISCUIT MIX

Serves 6

2 cups flour
3 teaspoons baking powder
3/4 teaspoon salt
5 tablespoons shortening, divided

Sift the dry ingredients together in a bowl. Cut in 3 tablespoons of the shortening until the mixture is in fine grains. Then cut in the remaining shortening. Store the mix tightly covered in the refrigerator. Makes 2 cups.

Westways Cowboy Baking Powder Biscuits
2 cups biscuit mix
2/3 to 3/4 cup milk

Add the milk to the biscuit mix and stir in lightly with a fork. Either roll the dough out and cut with a biscuit cutter or, as Darrell does, drop the biscuits by spoonfuls onto an ungreased baking sheet. Bake at 425 degrees for 12 to 15 minutes. Makes 8 to 12 biscuits.

> Westways "Private" Resort Inn
> Darrell Trapp
> P.O. Box 41624
> Phoenix, Arizona 85080
> telephone: (602) 582-3868

"We generally have several cupfuls of my own biscuit mix in the refrigerator. We find it just as easy to double this recipe and use it a cup at a time."

Trapp suggests a cartoon in which an innkeeper is cooking breakfast, talking on the telephone giving information about the inn or taking reservation information, checking a guest out, giving another guest directions or suggestions on where to go for the day... all at the same time.... while trying to appear composed. And in the meantime, waiting for a chance to have that second cup of coffee and a moment of quiet.

This mix makes "melt in your mouth" biscuits. It is a real family pleaser, the judges report.

PEACH YOGURT BREAD

Serves 6 to 8

1 cup flour
1 cup whole wheat flour
2/3 cup brown sugar
1/4 cup whole bran cereal
1 teaspoon baking soda
1 teaspoon cinnamon
1 egg, beaten
1 6-ounce carton peach yogurt
1/4 cup milk
1/4 cup oil

Combine the dry ingredients in a large bowl. Mix the liquid ingredients in a small bowl. Add the liquid ingredients to the dry ingredients just to moisten. Pour the batter into a greased loaf pan. Bake at 350 degrees for 50 minutes or until a wooden toothpick inserted near the center comes out clean. Cool in the pan for 10 minutes. Serve warm or cool.

Grunberg Haus Bed and Breakfast
Christopher Sellers and Mark Frohman
RR 2, Box 1595
Route 100 South
Waterbury, Vermont 05676
telephone: (802) 244-7726

Christopher and Mark find that it is efficient to, "Clean as you go!" They use large bowls for mixing because it saves time cleaning up spills. They pour juices into glasses ahead of time and store them in the refrigerator on trays, so serving time is quicker and the glasses are chilled, too.

The judges think that this is an excellent quick bread recipe. It is very easy to prepare and makes a healthy, delicious loaf.

GAY'S BANANA ORANGE MUFFIN CAKE

Serves 6 to 8

1 1/2 cups flour
1 cup rolled oats, uncooked
1/3 cup brown sugar
1 tablespoon baking powder
1/2 teaspoon baking soda
1/4 teaspoon salt
2/3 cup mashed, ripe bananas
1/2 cup orange juice
1/3 cup melted butter
1 egg, beaten
1/2 teaspoon grated orange

Glaze:

1/2 cup powdered sugar
1 tablespoon orange juice
1/2 teaspoon grated orange

Preheat the oven to 400 degrees. Grease a springform or bundt pan. Combine the dry ingredients. Combine the remaining ingredients and add them to the dry ingredients, stirring until just moistened. Pour the batter into the prepared pan and bake 30 to 35 minutes or until golden brown. Cool the cake for 10 minutes and remove it from the pan. Combine the glaze ingredients and drizzle the glaze evenly over the warm cake.

Alexander's Inn
Carolyn Lee and Mary Jo Schneider
529 East Palace Avenue
Santa Fe, New Mexico 87501
telephone: (505) 986-1431

"For me," writes Carolyn, "breakfast preparation boils down to the basics: I love to begin my day quietly and gently, so I allow plenty of time to set up. The energy in which food is prepared is very important to me. Ours is prepared with love and patience. I give myself plenty of time in the morning to set a lovely table with fresh cut flowers from our garden. The guests are here to relax and 'mellow out' and so the entire ambience of the inn supports them in this."

KATHY'S GRAHAM BREAD

Serves 6 to 8

2 cups graham flour
1 cup white flour
1 cup brown sugar
1 teaspoon baking powder
1 teaspoon salt
2 tablespoons vinegar with enough milk to make 2 cups

Mix the graham flour, white flour, brown sugar, baking powder, and salt. Pour the milk vinegar mixture over the dry ingredients and stir to mix. Pour the batter into a greased loaf pan. Let it stand for 20 minutes. Bake at 350 degrees for 1 hour and 15 minutes or until done. Test for doneness with a toothpick.

Note: A light graham flour is needed. You may need to play with the flour available in your area. Try health food stores, if necessary. If the bread is heavier, reduce the graham flour. This is very good with Eggs Hersey.

Hersey House
Gail Orell and Lynn Savage
451 North Main Street
Ashland, Oregon 97520
telephone: (503) 482-4563

SAFFRON BUNS

Serves 10

2 cups flour
1 teaspoon baking powder
1/8 teaspoon salt
1/4 teaspoon ground saffron
1 cup butter
1 1/3 cups brown sugar
3 eggs
1 cup dried apricots, finely chopped
1 teaspoon rose water

Preheat the oven to 375 degrees. Grease 20 muffin cups and set them aside.

Sift the flour, baking powder, salt, and saffron into a medium sized bowl. In a large mixing bowl, cream the butter and brown sugar together with a wooden spoon until they are soft and creamy. Beat in the eggs, one at a time, adding a little of the flour mixture with each egg. Using a metal spoon, fold in the remaining flour mixture. Stir in the apricots and rose water.

Fill each muffin cup about half full with the batter. Bake for 15 to 20 minutes or until the buns are golden brown and spring back when pressed with a finger. Let the buns cool in the pan for 5 minutes. Turn them out on a wire rack to cool completely before serving.

Chestnut Charm Bed and Breakfast
Barbara and Bruce Stensvad
1409 Chestnut Street
Atlantic, Iowa 50022
telephone: (712) 243-5652

Coffeecakes

APPLE BUNDT CAKE

Serves 12

COFFEECAKE BLUE RIBBON BREAKFAST WINNER !!

3 cups flour
1/2 teaspoon salt
1 teaspoon baking soda
1 cup sugar
3 cups diced raw cooking apples (2 1/4 medium apples)
1 cup chopped nuts
2 eggs
3/4 cup oil
1 teaspoon vanilla

Topping:
1/4 cup melted butter
1/8 cup sugar
1 tablespoon light corn syrup
1 teaspoon vanilla
powdered sugar (optional)

    Sift together the flour, salt, soda, and sugar. Add the apples and nuts. Mix together the eggs, oil, and vanilla. Add the liquid ingredients to the dry ingredients and mix until well blended. Pour the batter into a greased and floured tube pan. (The mixture will resemble cookie dough.) Bake at 350 degrees for 1 hour and 15 minutes.
    Mix the topping ingredients until blended. Pour the topping over the hot cake in the pan, letting it drizzle down the sides. Let the coffeecake cool for about 30 minutes before taking it out of the pan. Dust the cake with powdered sugar if desired.

Mt. Ashland Inn
Elaine and Jerry Shanafelt
550 Mt. Ashland Road
Ashland, Oregon 97520
telephone: (503) 482-8707

BREAKFAST APPLE CAKE

Serves 10 to 12

2 cups sugar
3 eggs
1 1/4 cup salad oil
1/4 teaspoon salt
1/4 cup orange juice
3 cups flour
1 teaspoon baking soda
1 teaspoon cinnamon
1 teaspoon vanilla
1 1/2 cups peeled and chopped apples
1 cup coconut
1 cup chopped nuts

    Mix the sugar and eggs. Add the oil, salt, and orange juice and stir until well blended. Sift the flour, baking soda, and cinnamon and blend into the sugar mixture. Stir in the vanilla. Add the apples, coconut, and nuts. Pour the batter into a greased and floured tube pan. Bake at 325 degrees for about 1 1/2 hours. Check for doneness at 1 1/4 hours. When ALMOST done, make the sauce.

Sauce:
6 tablespoons melted butter
1 cup sugar
1/2 teaspoon baking soda
1/2 cup buttermilk

    Mix the ingredients in a saucepan. Bring to a rolling boil. Pour it over the HOT cake still in the pan. Let the cake stand at least one hour before turning it out of the pan.

A Bed and Breakfast
Gary and Vi Savard
Star Route 62 #549
Center Harbor, New Hampshire 03226
telephone: (603)253-6151

This is an especially good coffee cake. It is hearty and moist. The apple, nut, and coconut combination is great, and the sauce soaks through to give a delicious flavor.

VIENNESE CRESCENT RING

Serves 8

1 cup ground almonds
1/3 cup powdered sugar
2 tablespoons margarine
1 teaspoon almond extract
1 egg separated

Combine the above ingredients using only the egg yolk. Set aside the egg white.

2 (8 ounce) cans quick crescent dinner rolls
2/3 cup apricot or peach preserves
1/4 cup sliced almonds
1 tablespoon sugar

Separate 1 can of dough into 8 triangles. Place the wide side of the triangles to the edge of a 12" pizza pan. Seal the perforations.

Separate the remaining can of dough into 8 triangles. Spread 1 tablespoon of the almond filling over each triangle. Roll very loosely and arrange around the edge of the pan.

Spoon the preserves over the center of the dough and around the sides of the filled crescents. Beat the egg white until it is frothy. Brush the tops of the filled crescents with the egg white. Sprinkle the tops with almonds and sugar. Bake at 350 degrees for 25 to 30 minutes.

Rancho San Gregorio
Bud and Lee Raynor
5086 LaHonda Road
Rt.1 Box 54
San Gregorio, California 94074

This recipe is a real favorite of the judges. It is easy to prepare and makes an elegant coffee cake hot from the oven.

PUMPKIN COFFEE CAKE

Serves 10

1/2 cup butter or margarine
3/4 cup sugar
1 teaspoon vanilla
3 eggs
2 cups flour
1 teaspoon baking powder
1 teaspoon baking soda
1 cup sour cream

filling:
1 3/4 cup pumpkin
1 egg
1/3 cup sugar
1 teaspoon pumpkin pie spice

streusel:
1 cup brown sugar
1/3 cup softened butter
2 teaspoons cinnamon
1 cup chopped nuts

Cream the butter, sugar, and vanilla in a mixing bowl. Add the eggs, beating well after each. Combine the flour, baking powder, and baking soda in another bowl. Add the dry ingredients alternately with the sour cream to the butter mixture.

To make the filling, combine the pumpkin, beaten egg, sugar, and pie spice.

To prepare the streusel, cut the brown sugar and butter together. Add the cinnamon and stir until blended. Stir in the chopped nuts.

Spoon half the batter into a greased 9" X 13" baking dish, spreading the batter to the corners. Sprinkle half the streusel over the batter. Spread the pumpkin mixture over the streusel. Carefully spread the remaining batter over the pumpkin mixture. Sprinkle the remaining streusel over the top. Bake at 325 degrees for 50 to 60 minutes.

Varns Guest House
Carl and Diane Eash
205 South Main Street
Middlebury, Indiana 46540
telephone: (219) 825-9666

The Eashes keep cereals in glass jars with a serving ladle for each variety. Each jar is labeled with the type of cereal. The jars keep the cereals fresh so the cereals can be purchased in larger, more economical boxes. This is also a more attractive way to set up the breakfast buffet.

FRESH FRUIT BREAKFAST CAKE   Serves 4 to 6

1 cup sugar
6 tablespoons butter, softened
1 egg
1 cup flour
1/2 teaspoon baking soda
1/2 teaspoon allspice
1/2 teaspoon cinnamon
1/2 teaspoon freshly grated nutmeg
1/8 teaspoon salt
2 cups fruit (peeled and cored apples, unpeeled nectarines, or peaches, or any combination)
1/2 cup almonds

Preheat the oven to 350 degrees. Butter or spray an 8" square or an oblong baking pan. Combine the sugar, butter, and egg in a large bowl and mix well with a wooden spoon. Add the flour, baking soda, spices, and salt and mix well. Fold in the fruit and nuts. Spoon into the prepared pan. Bake for 30 to 45 minutes until the top is browned and a toothpick inserted in the center comes out clean. Serve immediately.

The Cottage
Carol and Robert Emerick
3829 Albatross Street
San Diego, California 92103
telephone: (619) 299-1564

Carol Emerick writes, "Having a very small kitchen has turned out to be a blessing. I have a corner where I can stand and reach all my baking equipment, spices, and ingredients as well as load and unload the dish washer. This saves time in the long run."

GRANDMA FLICK'S BLUEBERRY COFFEE CAKE

Serves 12

2 cups flour
1 1/2 cup sugar
3/4 cup butter (1 1/2 sticks)

    Blend the above ingredients with a pastry blender until course. Reserve 1 cup for topping.

    To the remaining mixture, add:
2 teaspoons baking powder
1 cup milk
1 teaspoon vanilla
2 eggs
1/2 teaspoon salt

    Blend together and spread in a greased and floured 9" X 13" baking pan. Sprinkle 1 cup fresh or 1 can drained blueberries on top. Sprinkle with the reserved topping. Bake at 350 degrees for 30 minutes or until golden brown. Sprinkle with powdered sugar while hot.

Farm Fortune Bed and Breakfast
Chad and Phyllis Combs
204 Linekiln Road
New Cumberland, Pennsylvania 17070
telephone: (717) 774-2683

RASPBERRY CREAM CHEESE COFFEE CAKE

Serves 6 to 8

1 3 ounce package cream cheese
1/4 cup margarine or butter
2 cups packaged biscuit mix
1/4 cup milk
1/2 cup raspberry preserves

Icing:
1 cup sifted powdered sugar
1 to 2 tablespoons milk
1/2 teaspoon vanilla

In a bowl, cut the cream cheese and the margarine or butter into the biscuit mix until crumbly. Stir in 1/4 cup milk. Turn onto a lightly floured surface and knead 8 to 10 strokes.

On waxed paper, roll the dough to a 12" X 8" rectangle. Invert the dough onto a greased baking sheet. Remove the waxed paper. Spread the preserves down the center of the dough. Make 2 1/2 inch long cuts at 1 inch intervals along the sides. Fold the strips over the filling.

Bake the coffee cake at 375 degrees for about 20 minutes or until golden brown. Let cool for 5 minutes before frosting.

Mix the confectioners' sugar, milk, and vanilla in a small bowl. Drizzle the icing over the slightly cooled coffee cake and serve warm.

Chestnut Charm Bed and Breakfast
Barbara and Bruce Stensvad
1409 Chestnut Street
Atlantic, Iowa 50022

Yeast Breads

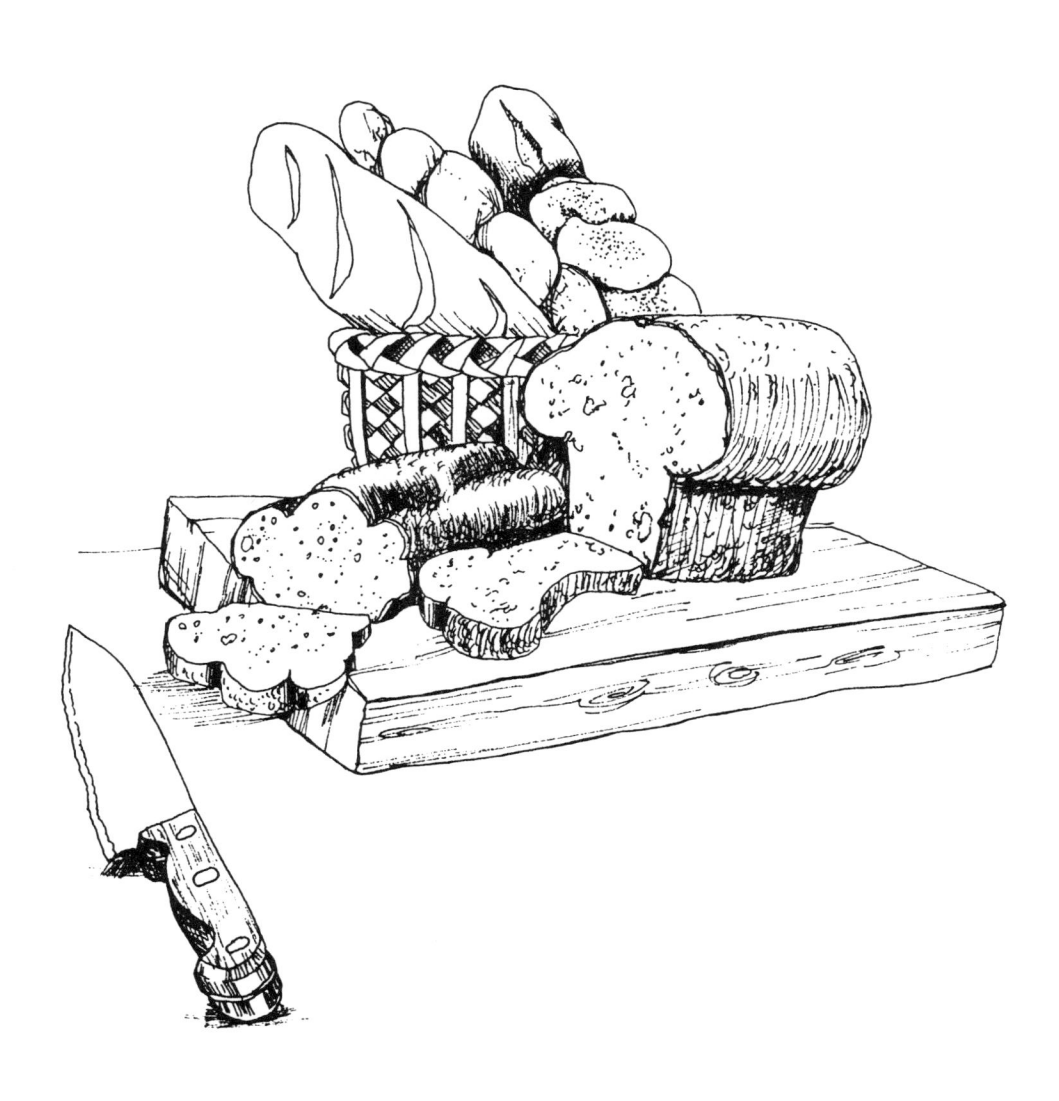

APPLEBUTTER SWEET ROLLS

Makes 2 dozen rolls

YEAST BREAD BLUE RIBBON BREAKFAST WINNER !!

1 package dry yeast
1/4 cup warm water
1 tablespoon brown sugar
1 3/4 cups scalded milk
1/4 cup sugar
1 teaspoon salt
1 egg, beaten
7 cups flour
3 teaspoons melted shortening

Filling:

2 cups applebutter
1/2 teaspoon cinnamon

Glaze:

2 cups powdered sugar
4 tablespoons milk
3/4 teaspoon vanilla

Dissolve the yeast in 1/4 cup warm water with 1 tablespoon brown sugar and let the mixture stand for 5 minutes.

Let the scalded milk cool to luke warm in a large mixing bowl. Add the 1/4 cup sugar, salt, yeast mixture, and beaten egg. Sift the flour and add 3 1/2 cups of flour, beating well. Add the melted shortening and thoroughly mix in the remaining flour. Cover the bowl with a moist towel and set it in a warm place away from drafts. Let the dough rise until double in size.

Divide the dough in half. Roll one half of the dough into a large rectangle 1/2" thick on a floured surface. Spread it with 1 cup of the applebutter and cinnamon filling. Roll the dough up and cut it into 1" slices, spacing the rolls about 2" apart on a greased baking pan. Repeat these steps with the other half of the dough. Cover the rolls with plastic wrap and refrigerate overnight.

In the morning, remove the rolls from the refrigerator and remove the plastic wrap. Let the rolls rise 1 hour and bake them at 350 degrees for 25 minutes. Glaze and serve warm.

Applebutter Inn
Gary and Sandra McKnight
666 Centreville Pike
Slippery Rock, Pennsylvania 16057
telephone: (412) 794-1844

This recipe was developed by the inn chef, Lynda Moore, especially for the Applebutter Inn. Breakfasts are served to guests in an original one room schoolhouse built in 1899 which is adjacent to the inn.

MARY YODER'S YUMMY CINNAMON ROLLS

Makes 24 rolls

1 cup water (lukewarm)
2 1/2 tablespoons yeast
1 teaspoon sugar
1 cup milk (warm)
1/2 cup oil
1/2 cup sugar
1 1/2 teaspoons salt
2 eggs (beaten)
1/2 teaspoon nutmeg
6 to 7 1/2 cups flour

filling:
1 tablespoon melted butter
1 cup brown sugar
2 tablespoons cinnamon

frosting:
1/2 cup margarine
2 1/2 cups powdered sugar
1/2 teaspoon vanilla
1/3 cup milk

In a small bowl, mix the water, yeast, and 1 teaspoon sugar.

In a very large bowl, combine the yeast mixture and the remaining ingredients. Mix by hand to make a workable, soft dough and knead for 3 to 5 minutes. Cover and let rise until double.

Roll the dough on a floured surface to make a 12"X 18" rectangle. Brush the dough with melted butter. Spread brown sugar evenly over the top. Sprinkle cinnamon over the brown sugar.

Roll up the dough jelly roll fashion and brush the edge with water to seal. Cut one inch slices and place them in greased 11" X 14" pans. Let the rolls rise until they are a little more than doubled. Bake at 350 degrees for 20 to 25 minutes.

To make the frosting, beat the ingredients for 5 to 10 minutes or until fluffy. Ice the cinnamon rolls while they are slightly warm.

Varns Guest House
Carl and Diane Eash
205 South Main Street
Middlebury, Indiana 46540
telephone: (219) 825-9666

These cinnamon rolls are made by Mary Yoder at Yoder's Restaurant in Goshen, Indiana. She shared her recipe, cut down to a more manageable size, with the Eashes.

SOUR CREAM BREAD ROLL

Serves 16

1 cup sour cream
1/2 cup sugar
1 teaspoon salt
1/2 cup margarine
2 packages dry yeast
1 teaspoon sugar
1/2 cup warm water
2 eggs, beaten
4 cups flour

filling:

2 8 ounce packages cream cheese
3/4 cup sugar
1 egg beaten
2 teaspoons vanilla or almond extract
1/8 teaspoon salt

glaze:

2 cups powdered sugar
2 teaspoons almond or vanilla extract
4 tablespoons milk

Heat the sour cream in a saucepan and stir in the 1/2 cup sugar, salt, and margarine until dissolved. Cool to lukewarm. In a small bowl, sprinkle the yeast into the warm water and add 1 teaspoon sugar. Let the yeast mixture rise and then add it to the sour cream mixture. Stir the eggs and flour into the sour cream mixture with a spoon. Store the dough overnight in the refrigerator in a covered container.

To make the filling, beat the softened cream cheese with the rest of the ingredients until smooth.

Divide the dough into four parts and roll each part into an 8" X 12" rectangle. Spread one fourth of the filling on each rectangle and roll up jelly roll fashion. Transfer the rolled up dough to a greased baking sheet. Slit each roll at 2 inch intervals two thirds of the way through. Cover and let rise for 1 hour. Bake at 375 degrees for 12 to 15 minutes. Frost while warm.

To make the frosting, combine the powdered sugar, vanilla, and milk in a small bowl and stir.

Varns Guest House
Carl and Diane Eash
205 South Main Street
Middlebury, Indiana 46540
telephone: (219) 825-9666

"The most important thing is to be hospitable," writes Diane's mother who serves breakfast at the inn.

REFRIGERATOR COFFEE CAKE

Serves 10 to 12

1/2 ounce yeast
2 tablespoons plus 1/4 teaspoon sugar
1 cup warm milk
3 1/2 cups flour
1/2 teaspoon salt
1 cup plus 1 teaspoon butter
2 egg yolks, slightly beaten
1 egg white

Filling:
1/2 cup sugar
1 cup raisins
1/2 cup almonds, halved

Icing:
1 cup confectioners' sugar
3 to 4 tablespoons water

Put the yeast in a large mixing bowl with 2 tablespoons of sugar and the warm milk. Stir constantly until the mixture is smooth. Sift in 1 cup of the flour and blend well. Cover and set the bowl aside in a warm draft free place for 1 hour.

Carefully add the remaining flour, the rest of the sugar, and the salt. With your hands, mix and knead the dough until it is smooth. Gradually work in 1 cup of the soft butter and the egg yolks. When both have been mixed in well, form the dough into a ball. Cover the bowl with a cloth and place it in the refrigerator to rise for 8 hours or overnight.

In the morning, remove the dough from the refrigerator and divide it into 2 equal parts. On a lightly floured surface, roll out each half into a rectangle about 12" X 20". With a pastry brush, coat one rectangle with a little of the egg white. Sprinkle on the 1/2 cup sugar and raisins. Place the other piece of dough on top. Roll up the sandwiched dough pieces and press the edges together to seal.

Lightly grease a large baking sheet with the remaining teaspoon of butter. Transfer the dough roll to the baking sheet and set it aside in a warm draft free place. Leave it for 2 1/2 to 3 hours or until the dough has risen and almost doubled in bulk.

Preheat the oven to 350 degrees. With a pastry brush, coat the dough roll with the remaining egg white. Stick the almond halves into the dough roll. Bake for 45 minutes to 1 hour or until the coffee cake is done and lightly browned all over.

Cool the coffee cake on a wire cooling rack. Sift the confectioners' sugar into a small bowl and stir in enough water to make a smooth icing. On a serving plate, trickle the icing over the cooled cake. Allow the icing to set before serving. Makes one 2 pound cake.

Chestnut Charm Bed and Breakfast
Barbara and Bruce Stensuad
1409 Chestnut Street
Atlantic, Iowa 50022
telephone: (712) 243-5652

COLONIAL BREAD FROM 1650

Makes 1 large loaf

Starter:
3 cups whole wheat flour
2 tablespoons yeast
3 cups warm water

The night before, mix the above ingredients in a large bowl. Cover the bowl with a damp towel and leave it in a warm place to sit for 8 to 12 hours before mixing the dough.

3 cups bread flour
2 cups unbleached flour
2 tablespoons salt
warm water

The next day, add the starter to the flours and salt. Add enough warm water to make a stiff dough. Knead the dough well. Put the dough in a greased bowl and cover it with a moist tea towel. Let the dough rise for 2 hours in a warm place. Punch down the dough and place it in a greased baking pan (the innkeepers recommend a round greased wedding-cake tin with the sides made higher with a 6" aluminum foil flashing). Cover the pan with a moist tea towel and let the dough rise in a warm place for 1 hour. Preheat the oven to 450 degrees and bake the bread for 30 minutes. Remove the bread from the pan and bake another 30 minutes at 300 degrees.

Newport House
Cathy and John Millar
710 South Henry Street
Williamsburg, Virginia 23185-4113
telephone: (804) 229-1775

To fashion a large baking pan, the judge used a large iron skillet with higher sides of tin foil. This is an impressive, large loaf of delicious bread.

OATMEAL APPLE BREAD

Makes 3 loaves

1/3 cup raisins
2 tablespoons rum

1/3 cup brown sugar
1 teaspoon white sugar
2 tablespoons molasses
1/2 cup warm apple juice (110 F or 45 C)
1 1/3 cups unsweetened apple juice or apple cider
1 tablespoon salt
2 tablespoons melted butter

2 packages active dry yeast
5 1/2 to 6 cups bread flour
1/2 teaspoon cinnamon

1 1/2 cups rolled oats
3/4 cup finely chopped apple (use grating blade on food processor)
1/2 cup chopped walnuts

1 egg white blended with 1 tablespoon water

    In a small bowl, mix the raisins and rum. Cover and set aside 3 to 4 hours or overnight.
    In a heavy sauce pan, mix the brown and white sugars with the molasses, salt, 1/2 cup apple juice, 1 1/3 cups unsweetened apple juice or cider, and butter. Heat until warm.
    In a large bowl, mix 3 cups of the bread flour with the cinnamon and yeast. Add the warm liquid mixture and mix well. Add the oats, chopped apple, nuts, and soaked raisins and mix well. Add enough of the remaining flour to make a soft dough.
    Turn the dough onto a lightly floured surface. Knead the dough 8 to 10 minutes or until it is smooth and elastic. Place the dough in a large greased bowl, turning to coat all sides. Cover the bowl and let the dough rise until double in a warm, moist oven.
    After about an hour, punch down the dough and knead it for 30 seconds. Divide the dough into thirds, shape it into loaves, and place it into 3 greased loaf pans. Let the dough rise again until double in a warm, moist oven.
    In about an hour, gently remove the pans from the oven and preheat the oven to 375 degrees. Brush the loaves with the egg white and water glaze. Bake for 35 to 40 minutes or until the bread sounds hollow with tapped on the bottom of the pan. If the bread is browning too quickly, put a foil tent over it. When baked, remove the loaves from the pans and cool them on racks.

Chestnut Charm Bed and Breakfast
Barbara Stensvad
1409 Chestnut Street
Atlantic, Iowa 50022
telephone: (712) 243-5652

QUICK EGG BREAD

Makes 2 loaves or 24 rolls

3 to 4 cups bread flour
2 envelopes fast rising dry yeast
1 cup hot water
1 1/2 teaspoons salt
2 tablespoons sugar
2 tablespoons cooking oil
2 eggs

Combine 1 1/2 cups flour with the yeast. Mix thoroughly. In a small pan, heat the hot water, salt, sugar, and oil until just warm when stirred with a finger. Add the water mixture to the flour and mix well. Add the eggs one at a time, mixing well with an electric mixer. Using a wooden spoon, add just enough flour to make a ball that is not sticky. Knead the dough on a floured surface. Add a little flour as necessary and knead until the dough is smooth and makes bubbles.

Place the dough in a greased bowl and put it in a warm oven with a pot of boiling water. Let the dough rise until it doubles. Take the dough out of the oven and cut it into rolls or make 2 loaves. Put the loaves or rolls into greased pans and return them to the warm, moist oven to rise until doubled. Butter or egg wash the tops. Bake at 350 degrees for about 20 minutes or until done.

Chestnut Charm Bed and Breakfast
Barbara Stensvad
1409 Chestnut Street
Atlantic, Iowa 50022
telephone: (712) 243-5652

BREAD FOR THE BUSY INNKEEPER

Makes 1 loaf

3 1/2 cups flour
2 tablespoons sugar
1/2 teaspoon salt
1 package quick rise yeast
2 tablespoons oil
1 1/3 cups hot water (125 to 130 degrees)

Mix the flour, sugar, salt, and yeast. Add the oil and water. Stir to make a thick, WET dough. Cover and let rise until double, about 30 minutes. Stir the dough down and pour it into a 9" X 5" X 3" loaf pan. Cover the pan with a damp towel. Let the dough rise until double. Bake the bread at 375 degrees for 35 minutes.

To make raisin bread, add 3/4 cup raisins to the flour mixture. Add 1 to 2 teaspoons cinnamon when you stir the dough down, so it will stay in the dough in streaks. Glaze if desired while the bread is still warm, but not hot.

Lavender Inn Bed and Breakfast
Rose Degni and Lyn Daring
RR #1 Box 325
Seneca Turnpike East
Vernon, New York 13476
telephone: (315) 829-2440

Rose and Lyn always keep some frozen baked goods on hand. They also keep frozen quiche, souffle, and French toast for unexpected late arrival guests.

They cook bacon lightly the night before in the microwave, cover it with plastic wrap and refrigerate it, and finish cooking it in the morning.

To make breakfast look most attractive, they vary the china and handwoven or quilted placemats each day. Rose and Lyn use some of the pitchers from their collection, too.

Mint leaves and edible flowers such as johnny-jump-ups, calendulas, nasturtiums, and chive flowers are often used for garnishes.

The judges thought that this bread recipe was fast and easy to prepare. The bread is very tasty.

LINDA'S BREAD

Makes 1 loaf

1 tablespoon (1 packet) dry yeast
1 tablespoon sugar
1 cup warm water (105 to 115 degrees)
3 tablespoons oil
1 teaspoon salt
3 tablespoons brown sugar
1/3 cup dry milk powder
3/4 cup whole wheat flour
3/4 cup bran cereal
3/4 cup rolled oats
3/4 cup bread flour

In a small bowl, dissolve the yeast and 1 tablespoon sugar in warm water. Set the mixture aside while assembling the other ingredients.

Beat together in a large bowl the dissolved yeast, oil, salt, brown sugar and dry milk. Stir in the mixed grains, adding the bread flour last.

Turn the dough out on a lightly floured board and knead for 10 to 15 minutes, incorporating as little extra flour as possible. Place the dough in a greased bowl. Cover it with a towel or plastic wrap and set it in a warm area away from drafts. Let the dough rise 1 1/2 hours.

Punch the dough down and knead briefly. Cover the dough and let it rise again for about 1 hour.

Punch the dough down and place it on a clean, lightly floured surface. Flatten the dough into a 6" X 12" rectangle. Starting with the 6 inch side, roll the dough in a jelly roll fashion, stretching the dough slightly to help eliminate air bubbles. Tuck the ends under and place the dough in a greased loaf pan, seam side down.

Bake in a 425 degree oven for 10 minutes. Reduce the temperature to 375 degrees and bake for 30 minutes or until the bread is browned and sounds hollow when tapped. Remove the bread from the pan and cool on a wire rack. Wrap in foil when cool.

Grandview Lodge
Stan and Linda Arnold
809 Valley View Circle Road
Waynesville, North Carolina 28786
telephone: (704) 456-5212

Since this bread has no preservatives, it will not keep long at room temperature. Linda suggests that you slice the bread and store it in the freezer. Then you can thaw as many slices as you need.

Pancakes & Waffles

FOUR BERRY PANCAKES

Serves 4 to 6

PANCAKES/WAFFLES BLUE RIBBON BREAKFAST WINNER !!

1 1/2 cups flour
2 tablespoons sugar
1 teaspoon salt
1 teaspoon baking powder
3 tablespoons oil
2 eggs
1/2 cup plain yogurt
3/4 cup milk
3 cups fresh berries in any combination desired
(blueberries, raspberries, strawberries, blackberries)

Mix all the dry ingredients, mix all the wet ingredients, and combine to make the pancake batter. Reserve 2 cups of fruit and add the rest to the batter. Pour 1/4 cup batter per pancake on a hot, oiled griddle. Turn the pancakes when the edges are dry and bubbles appear. Arrange 3 pancakes on a plate per person. Top with a scoop of Ben and Jerry's vanilla ice cream, 1/2 cup fruit and hot Vermont maple syrup. Add a sprig of fresh mint to garnish.

> Pam and Gary Gosselin
> Inn at Blush Hill
> Blush Hill Road, Box 1266
> Waterbury, Vermont 05676
> telephone: (802) 244-752

To save time when making the pancake batter, Pam and Gary mix the wet ingredients and the dry ingredients separately the night before. Then they mix the batter in the morning.

"As a specialty of the house we top all pancakes and French toast with a scoop of Ben and Jerry's ice cream. We are located next to the Ben and Jerry's original factory and tourist center!"

BETTY'S BUTTERMILK PANCAKES
A LA STRAWBERRIES

Serves 4 to 6

2 cups flour
2 tablespoons sugar
2 heaping teaspoons baking powder
2 teaspoons baking soda
2 cups buttermilk (lowfat if desired)
2 eggs
4 tablespoons corn oil

Combine the first four ingredients in a large bowl. Combine the last three ingredients in a measuring cup and add to the dry ingredients. Blend until the flour is moistened and well mixed, but still lumpy. DO NOT BEAT. Wait a few minutes. Drop the batter onto a hot griddle (325 to 350 degrees) with a 1/4 cup measuring cup. Cook until the edges begin to dry and bubbles appear. Flip and cook until set.

Serve with fresh strawberries, cut up and mixed with sugar to taste. Arrange three pancakes on a plate. Spread strawberries in the center. Top with whipped cream and place a strawberry on top.

Frank and Jo Davis
Harrington House Bed and Breakfast
5626 Gulf Drive
Holmes Beach, Florida 34217

Jo prepares the pancake mix in advance by measuring the dry ingredients into a plastic container. She can make several batches. When she is ready to make pancakes, she shakes the container to blend the ingredients, puts the mix into a bowl, and adds the liquid ingredients.

Frank and Jo offer coffee and poppy seed cake, or muffins for early breakfast-to-go.

LEMON RICOTTA PANCAKES　　　　　　　　　　Serves 4 to 6

3/4 cup flour
1 teaspoon baking powder
1/2 teaspoon nutmeg
2 eggs
1 cup ricotta cheese (7 1/2 to 8 ounces)
2/3 cup milk
1 tablespoon sugar
juice and grated peel of one lemon

　　Mix the flour, baking powder, and nutmeg in a large bowl. Mix the eggs, ricotta cheese, milk, sugar, and lemon juice and peel in a medium bowl. Add the egg mixture to the flour mixture and blend until smooth. Pour 1/3 cup of the batter onto a hot, greased griddle. Spread the batter into a 5 inch circle. Cook until the pancake is golden, turning once. Arrange the pancakes on a platter and dust with powdered sugar. Serve with Vermont maple syrup. Makes 14 pancakes.

　　　　　　　　　　Christopher Sellers and Mark Frohman
　　　　　　　　　　Grunberg Haus Bed and Breakfast
　　　　　　　　　　RR 2, Box 1595, Route 100 South
　　　　　　　　　　Waterbury, Vermont 05676
　　　　　　　　　　telephone: (802) 244-7726

BAVARIAN PANCAKE

Serves 4

1/3 cup flour
1/3 cup milk
1/4 teaspoon baking powder
2 large eggs
2 tablespoons margarine
1 21 ounce can apple pie filling
1 cup grated Cheddar cheese

Preheat the oven to 400 degrees. Mix the flour, milk, baking powder and eggs. Leave the batter lumpy. Melt the butter in a 10 inch baking dish. Pour in the batter. Bake 15 minutes. Heat the pie filling. Top the pancake with half the cheese, the heated apples, and the remaining cheese. Bake until the cheese melts.

Fran and Rich Oliver
Trestle House Inn
Soundside Road
P.O. RT 4, Box 370
Edenton, North Carolina 27932
telephone: (919) 482-2282

Fran and Rich serve fresh fruit on long wooden picks to garnish their entrees. An early morning breakfast-to-go is fresh fruit, muffins, juice, and tea or coffee.

TAYLOR'S STORE WHOLE-GRAIN PANCAKES

Serves 2 to 4

No Cholesterol

1 cup "Stoneground" whole wheat or rye flour
2 tablespoons sugar
2 tablespoons baking powder
1 teaspoon allspice
1/4 teaspoon nutmeg
2 egg whites, whipped slightly
1 cup skim milk
2 tablespoons sunflower or safflower oil

Combine the first 5 ingredients. Whip the egg whites slightly, and combine them well with the dry ingredients. Add milk and oil at the same time. Allow the batter to "rise" for at least 20 minutes. Spray the griddle with oil. If desired, you may add nuts or fruit to the pancakes after they are poured on the griddle. Makes 8 to 10 pancakes or 2 large portions.

Mary Lynn and Lee Tucker
The Manor at Taylor's Store
Rt 1, Box 533
South Mountain Lake, Virginia 24184
telephone: (703) 721-3951

Mary Ann Tucker writes, "This is a completely original recipe, developed by my husband, Lee, who is a physician on a no cholesterol campaign."

WHOLE GRAIN PANCAKES

Serves 4

1/2 cup yellow cornmeal
1/2 cup whole wheat flour
1/2 cup rolled oats
1 tablespoon baking powder
1/4 teaspoon baking soda
1 tablespoon sugar
1 to 1 1/2 cups buttermilk
1 egg
1/3 cup oil

In a large mixing bowl, combine all the dry ingredients. In a small bowl, beat together the 1 cup buttermilk, egg and oil. Beat the milk mixture into the dry ingredients and mix well. Add more buttermilk if the batter thickens while standing.

Pour 1/3 cup of the batter for each pancake onto a lightly oiled, medium hot griddle. Turn the pancakes before the bubbles burst. Serve immediately. To reduce sugar, these pancakes may be topped with fresh fruit or unsweetened applesauce.

Stan and Linda Arnold
Grandview Lodge
809 Valley Circle Road
Waynesville, North Carolina 28786
telephone: (704) 456-5212

APPLE WALNUT WHOLE WHEAT PANCAKES

Serves 3 to 4

2/3 cup milk
2 tablespoons melted butter or margarine
2 tablespoons molasses
1 egg
2/3 cup flour
1/3 cup whole wheat flour
2 teaspoons baking powder
1/4 teaspoon salt
1/4 cup chopped walnuts
1/2 medium green apple, peeled and diced

Beat the milk, butter, molasses and egg together lightly. Sift the flours, baking powder, and salt together. Add the nuts and apple to the flour mixture. Add the flour mixture all at once to the milk mixture and stir just enough to dampen the batter. Add more milk, if necessary, to make a batter about as thick as heavy cream. Cook on a hot griddle. Makes 10 to 12 four inch pancakes.

Mt Ashland Inn
Elaine and Jerry Shanafelt
550 Mt. Ashland Road
Ashland, Oregon 97520
telephone: (503) 482-8707

The Shanafelts keep juices and milk in a guest refrigerator in the dining room. For early risers they put homemade granola on the dining room buffet. They wrap breakfast breads or muffins and label them with the guests' names. These are left on the buffet or in the guests' room. They either get up to brew fresh coffee or put it in a carafe or the guests' thermos the night before.

COLONIAL NEWPORT JONNYCAKES   Serves 2 to 4

1 cup Jonnycake Meal
1 tablespoon sugar
1/2 teaspoon salt
1 cup boiling water
3 tablespoons milk
2 tablespoons rum

Combine the sugar, salt, and cornmeal in a large mixing bowl. Add the boiling water and stir well. Thin immediately with milk and rum, so the mixture will drop easily from the spoon. (You may need additional rum. The mixture should be the consistency of thin mashed potatoes.) Drop by spoonfuls onto a 350 to 400 degree griddle, very well greased. Do not let the griddle get dry. Cook 5 to 6 minutes on each side until a brown, crunchy crust is formed and the inside is cooked. Serve the Jonnycakes with butter and molasses.

Cathy and John Millar
Newport House
710 South Henry Street
Williamsburg, Virginia 23185-4113
telephone (804) 229-1775

Cathy and John Millar explain, "The Newport House is a copy of a 1756 house in Newport, Rhode Island that was torn down on its 200th birthday to make a car-park, so we thought we ought to have at least one historic Newport, Rhode Island recipe for our guests.

"Rhode Island Jonnycakes (no "h" in the spelling, as it was once "Journeycakes") used to contain rum, but you never see it mentioned in recipes today. The British reaction to Rhode Islanders smuggling molasses to make rum was a cause of the Revolution!"

BANANA BUTTERMILK BUCKWHEAT PANCAKES

Serves 4

1/3 cup whole-wheat flour
1/3 cup buckwheat flour
1/3 cup all-purpose flour
1/2 teaspoon baking soda
1/4 teaspoon salt
2 teaspoons baking powder
1 tablespoon sugar
1 ripe banana, mashed
1 egg
1 cup buttermilk
2 tablespoons oil
maple syrup

In a bowl, stir together the flours, soda, salt, baking powder, and sugar. In another bowl, whisk together the banana, egg, buttermilk, and oil. Whisk the banana mixture into the flour mixture until the batter is combined well. Heat a griddle over moderately high heat until it is hot enough to make drops of water scatter over its surface. Brush it with melted butter or oil. Drop the batter onto the griddle by 1/4 cup measures and cook the pancakes on each side until they are golden. Serve the pancakes with maple syrup.

Mary Davies
10 Inverness Way
Inverness, California 94937
telephone: (415) 669-1648

Mary serves baked grapefruit on her collection of antique flowered China saucers. She likes to garnish breakfasts with herbs and flowers from her garden. For example scrambled eggs with chives are topped with cheese and purple flowers from the chive plants.

An easy early breakfast-to-go is a fresh fruit cup, homemade coffeecake from the freezer, and a thermos of coffee.

COTTAGE CRÊPES

Serves 4

Crêpe Mixture:
1 cup cold water
1 cup milk
4 eggs
1/4 teaspoon salt
2 cups flour
4 tablespoons melted butter

Filling:
8 slices ham cut 1/8 inch thick
8 slices Swiss cheese cut 1/8 inch thick

Place the crêpe ingredients in a blender or food processor and blend until smooth. Refrigerate for at least two hours. Treat a non-stick frying pan or a crêpe pan with 1/4 teaspoon vegetable oil. Heat the pan on high heat. Pour 3 to 4 tablespoons of batter into the pan. Lift and tilt the pan in a circular motion to form a 6 inch crêpe. Brown on one side. Then flip the crêpe and lightly brown the other side. Remove the crêpe from the pan and let it cool. Stack the crêpes between layers of waxed paper. Repeat until all the batter is used. (Extra crêpes can be frozen for future use.)

Lightly grease a rectangular baking dish and set it aside. Preheat the oven to 375 degrees.

Taking one crêpe at a time, lay each on a flat surface. Place one slice of cheese and one slice of ham on the crêpe. Roll the filled crêpe tightly and place it seam side down in the baking dish. Continue with the rest of the crêpes. Bake for 10 to 13 minutes or until the cheese has melted. Serve immediately. Serve with Hollandaise sauce or with a dipping mustard.

The King's Cottage, A Bed and Breakfast Inn
Karen and Jim Owens
1049 East King Street
Lancaster, Pennsylvania 17602
telephone: (717) 397-1017

"We serve most dishes family style, so we garnish every dish before it goes to the table," Karen and Jim write. "A favorite garnish is kale topped with grapes and a sprig of parsley. We try to experiment and vary the garnish with the season."

One judge remarked that this recipe was "too formidable a task" for her current life style. She said this as an apology for not getting to test the recipe promptly, but her comment was extremely helpful. This recipe does take a long time to prepare. It was delicious and well received by the tasters. It could be prepared ahead and refrigerated overnight. However, this is not an easy, quick breakfast entree.

LEMON POPPY SEED WAFFLES

Serves 4

2 slightly beaten eggs
2 cups Bisquick mix
2 8 ounce cartons lemon yogurt
1/2 cup cooking oil
2 teaspoons poppy seed

Lightly grease the waffle iron and preheat. In a large bowl combine all the ingredients and stir until just slightly lumpy. Pour the necessary amount of batter onto the waffle iron and spread slightly. Bake 4 to 5 minutes until done. Serve hot with strawberry, blueberry, or maple syrup or garnish with lemon yogurt and finely grated lemon peel.

Ellen and Bucky Laufersweiler
Blushing Rose Bed and Breakfast
11 William Street
Hammondsport, New York 14840
telephone: (607) 589-3402

The Laufersweilers have found that their guests love breakfast at nine o'clock in the morning. For the rare guest who needs an early breakfast, they serve granola, juice, muffins, and coffee.

NORWEGIAN WAFFLES
Serves 4

5 eggs
1/2 cup sugar
1 teaspoon ground cardamom
3/4 cup sour cream
1 cup flour
1/4 cup melted butter

In a medium mixing bowl placed over a pan of hot water, beat the eggs and sugar together with a wire whisk or electric mixer until the mixture is thick and will form a ribbon trail on itself when the whisk is lifted.

With a metal spoon, stir in the cardamom and sour cream.

Fold in the flour, and when the mixture is smooth, stir in the melted butter.

Cover the bowl and set it aside to rest for 15 minutes.

Heat the waffle iron until it is very hot.

Pour some waffle mix on the center of the iron. Close the top and cook until the waffle is crisp and brown. Remove it from the waffle iron. Keep the waffle warm in the oven while the remaining waffles are being cooked. Makes about 6 waffles.

Barbara Stensvad
Chestnut Charm Bed and Breakfast
1409 Chestnut Street
Atlantic, Iowa 50022
telephone: (712) 243-5652

WHOLE WHEAT WAFFLES

Serves 4

1 cup milk
1 cup water
1/4 cup butter
1/4 cup honey
2 2/3 cups whole wheat flour
3 eggs
1 package dry yeast
1 1/2 teaspoons salt

Heat the water, milk, butter, and honey until the butter is melted (120 degrees). Put the mixture into a large mixing bowl. Add eggs, yeast, salt, and flour. Mix for one minute. Cover and refrigerate for several hours or overnight, stirring down occasionally. Be sure to use a large bowl, so the batter can double in volume. Preheat the waffle maker. Pour approximately 1/2 cup batter in the center of the waffle iron. Bake about three minutes. Serve with powdered sugar and butter.

Donna and Jerry Karson
Main Street Bed and Breakfast
403 E. Main Street
Harbor Springs, Michigan 49740
telephone: (616) 526-7782

The Karsons grow mint just outside the kitchen. Fresh mint leaves make lovely garnishes for fruit cups and melon wedges. Guests often like to add mint to their tea, too.

French Toast

BLUSHING ROSE'S FRENCH TOAST

Serves 6 to 8

1 loaf homemade or store baked raisin bread
6 eggs
1 1/2 cups milk
1 cup half and half
1 teaspoon vanilla
1/4 teaspoon cinnamon
1/4 teaspoon nutmeg
1/4 cup sugar
1/4 to 1/2 teaspoon cinnamon

Topping:
1/4 cup butter or margarine
1/2 cup brown sugar
1/2 cup chopped nuts (optional)

Slice the bread and arrange it in a buttered 9" X 13" baking dish by overlapping the slices lengthwise. Mix the eggs, milk, half and half, vanilla, cinnamon, and nutmeg. Pour the egg mixture over the bread and sprinkle the bread lightly with cinnamon and sugar. Cover and refrigerate overnight.

In the morning, mix the butter or margarine, brown sugar, and chopped nuts and sprinkle the mixture over the top of the bread. If desired, you may omit this topping. Bake at 350 degrees for about 40 minutes. Serve with hot syrup. Merry Berry Syrup is best. See the recipe in Condiments/Beverages chapter.

For a low cholesterol option use egg beaters and 2 1/2 cups skim milk.

This recipe can also be made substituting 1 cup of the half and half with 1 cup orange juice, 1 teaspoon vanilla, and 1 teaspoon orange flavoring. Omit the cinnamon and nutmeg.

Blushing Rose Bed and Breakfast
Ellen and Bucky Laufersweiler
11 William Street
Hammondsport, New York 14840
telephone: (607) 569-3402

COUNTRY FRENCH TOAST

Serves 4

1 loaf French bread
6 eggs
1 cup milk
1 teaspoon vanilla
1 teaspoon nutmeg (or less, to taste)
1 1/2 cups crushed corn flakes

    Slice the French bread diagonally into 1 1/2" thick slices. Beat the eggs, milk, vanilla, and nutmeg until well mixed. Place crushed corn flakes in a bowl. Dip the French bread into the egg mixture, then coat with the corn flakes. Dab butter onto a grill and brown both sides of the French toast. Serve with Maine blueberries in hot maple syrup.

Scotland Bridge Inn
Duke and Sylvia S. B. Jansen
One Scotland Bridge Road
York, Maine 03909
telephone: (207) 363-4432

In addition to setting the table the evening before, Duke and Sylvia also get out all the serving dishes that are to be used. "It is a great time saver!"

They use herbs, sliced tomatoes, or sliced fruits as garnishes. They also use a variety of lettuces to add color to the plates.

SUNNY PINES SURPRISE TOAST

Serves 12

12 slices French bread
cream cheese
jam or jelly
chopped pecans or almonds
12 eggs
2 cups milk

Syrup:

maple syrup
fresh fruit
1/4 cup butter
liquor of choice

Butterfly 12 slices of French bread. Spread cream cheese inside. Spread jam or jelly inside. Sprinkle chopped pecans or almonds inside and close the "sandwiches." Soak the "sandwiches" in 12 eggs beaten with 2 cups of milk. Fry on a greased griddle or bake in a buttered oven proof dish until golden brown on both sides. Serve with fresh fruit simmered in maple syrup and 1/4 cup butter and a dollop of a liquor of choice.

Cape Cod Sunny Pines Bed and Breakfast Inn
Eileen and Jack Connell
77 Main Street P.O. Box 667
Harwich, Maine 02671
telephone: (508) 432-9628

During harried moments, Eileen and Jack confess to having "whisper fights" where, as Eileen says, "words are passed with some anger and it is so ineffectual that we wind up with a great laugh."

To save time and to be more efficient, they have recently remodeled their kitchen. It now has two 30 inch gas stoves and a commercial refrigerator with glass doors. They bought all used equipment to economize. The changes have doubled their cooking area and reduced their "whisper fights."

The Connells emphasize their Irish backgrounds when serving their breakfasts. They serve family style and garnish the omelette plate with fried tomatoes, a very Irish custom. They like to serve colcannon with Irish mixed grille meats. Colcannon is made from potatoes, cabbage, and onion whipped together with cream and butter. To give guests a low calorie and low cholesterol choice they also serve Irish oatmeal with cranberry conserve (see Condiments/Beverages for the recipe) and bowls of fresh fruit.

BAKED FRENCH TOAST

Serves 6 to 8

Crusty French bread cut into 1/2 inch slices
6 eggs
1 1/2 cups milk
1 1/2 cups half and half
1 teaspoon vanilla
1 teaspoon cinnamon
3/4 cup slivered almonds

Arrange bread slices in a buttered 10" X 15" X 2" glass baking pan. Mix the remaining ingredients and pour over the bread slices. Sprinkle with 3/4 cup slivered almonds.

Topping:
1 stick butter or margarine, softened
1 cup brown sugar
1/4 cup maple syrup

Mix the topping ingredients together and sprinkle over the top of the bread slices. Cover and refrigerate overnight.

In the morning, bake uncovered for 40 minutes or until done at 350 degrees.

Captain Ezra Nye House
Elaine and Harry Dickson
152 Main Street
Sandwich, Maine 02563
telephone: (800) 388-2278, (508) 888-6142

Elaine Dickson writes, "We had a well known movie producer staying with us, and I was anxious for everything to come out especially nice. While I was fixing breakfast, he came into the kitchen, pulled up a stool, and struck up a conversation. Needless to say, I was a little flustered. As I was serving breakfast, the cheese souffle looked a little flat. When I tasted it, I realized I had left out the cheese!"

To avoid the early morning rush, Elaine says, "I make yeast coffee cakes and breads the night before and let them rise once. Then I put them in the refrigerator and bring them out the following morning for a second rising and baking." She uses a large pan for dirty dishes and utensils to keep the sink and counter tops uncluttered. Then she can wash everything at once after breakfast is prepared.

"We use Blue Willow table wear. It lends itself to a sea captain's home. Sometimes I serve by candlelight. For garnishes, I use mint and orange slices."

At the Captain Ezra Nye House, early rising guests have coffee or tea, fruit juice, and muffins "to go" for breakfast.

PEACHES AND CREAM FRENCH TOAST
Serves 4

6 slices French or Italian bread
3 eggs
1 cup light cream
2 tablespoons peach preserves
1/4 teaspoon nutmeg
1/4 to 1/2 teaspoon cinnamon
3 tablespoons melted butter
3 cups fresh, peeled, sliced peaches
confectioner's sugar

Cut the bread on the diagonal into 3/4" thick slices. Arrange the slices in a single layer in a greased baking pan. Combine the eggs, cream, peach preserves, nutmeg, and cinnamon. Beat the mixture until smooth and pour it over the bread. Turn the slices to coat evenly. Cover and refrigerate overnight. To cook, melt the butter in a skillet or grill. Remove the bread slices and saute in the heated pan until golden, about 5 minutes on each side. Top with fresh peaches and sprinkle with powdered sugar.

Five Gables Inn
Paul and Ellen Morissette
Murry Hill Road
East Boothbay, Maine 04544
telephone: (207) 633-4551

DUNSCROFT'S OWN BEST FRENCH TOAST EVER
Serves 10 to 12

1 quart light cream
3 tablespoons sugar
1/2 teaspoon vanilla extract
1/2 teaspoon almond extract
4 eggs
Challah bread

Mix the first five ingredients and beat until smooth.
Cut the Challah bread into 1 inch thick slices. Dip the slices into the egg mixture until partially absorbed. Grease the griddle with real butter. On low heat, toast the slices until lightly browned.

Dunscroft By-the-Sea Inn and Cottage
Alyce and Wally Cunningham
24 Pilgrim Road
Harwich Port, Maine 02646
telephone: (508) 432-0810

PLUMY FRENCH TOAST

Serves 4

plum jam
white or cinnamon bread
3 eggs
1/2 cup sour cream
1 teaspoon vanilla
melted butter
confectioner's sugar

Prepare a sandwich with thickly spread plum jam on good quality white or cinnamon bread. Dip the sandwich in a cream mixture made from the beaten eggs, cup sour cream, and vanilla. Drain and let stand for 10 minutes. Then fry the "sandwiches" in melted butter until golden brown. Sprinkle with confectioner's sugar before serving.

> The Inn at Manchester
> Stan and Harriet Rosenberg
> Rt 7A, Box 41
> Manchester, Vermont 05254
> telephone: (802) 362-1793

RICOTTA-STUFFED FRENCH TOAST
Serves 8 to 12

1 pound Italian bread
8 ounces ricotta cheese
4 eggs
1/2 cup cream
1 tablespoon vanilla
1/2 teaspoon nutmeg
1/2 teaspoon cinnamon

Cut the bread into 24 thin slices. Spread 12 slices with ricotta cheese. Top with the remaining 12 slices. Beat together the eggs, cream, vanilla, nutmeg, and cinnamon. Dip the bread and cheese "sandwiches" into the egg mixture. Grill slowly on a buttered griddle until browned. Dust with confectioner's sugar. Serve with Vermont maple sugar.

Grunberg Haus Bed and Breakfast
Christopher Sellers and Mark Frohman
RR 2 Box 1595 Route 100 South
Waterbury, Vermont 05676
telephone: (802) 244-7726

Christopher relates busy kitchen moments. "Mark and I share duties at breakfast. Our kitchen has a center island which we use as a sort of traffic circle—just like the European roadways. Our "exits" are the range, the dishwasher, the sink, the preparation counter, and the refrigerator. Even so, we hit "traffic jams" when he is coming in with used dishes and I am going out with quiche. We've considered, but not yet installed, a traffic signal."

Mark and Christopher serve a four course breakfast. The fruit, breads, and main dish courses are followed by a fat free, no calorie course of live piano music.

STUFFED FRENCH TOAST

Serves 10

2 French bread loaves 22 to 24 inches long
1 10 ounce jar fruit preserves
1 8 ounce package cream cheese
18 to 20 eggs
1/2 cup milk
2 teaspoons vanilla
1/2 teaspoon cinnamon
1/8 teaspoon nutmeg
butter flavored cooking spray
powdered sugar

Cut the bread into 2" slices. On the bottom edge of each piece, slice a pocket, leaving a 1/2" border on three sides. Fill the pockets with 1 teaspoon of jam. Slice the cream cheese into 1/2" thick slices and cut into 1" squares. Place a square of cream cheese into the jam filled pockets. Combine the next 5 ingredients and mix well. Let each side of the filled bread soak for 1 minute in the egg mixture and place on a hot griddle sprayed with a butter flavored cooking spray. Grill until brown. Place 2 pieces of French toast on each plate and sprinkle with powdered sugar.

For lower calorie alternatives, use low sugar jams and lite cream cheese.

The Cain House
Chris and Marachal Gohlich
11 Main Street
Bridgeport, California 93517
telephone: (619) 932-7040

Chris writes, "I do all the cooking and serving myself—not buffet style. Most people cannot believe that I serve fourteen people as easily as I do. All I can say is ORGANIZATION! The night before, I set all the tables, prepare the coffee, squeeze the O.J., and get out all of the cooking dishes and pans. I put all the plates in couples on the kitchen table. The next morning, I plug in the coffee and get to work. Two tips that I have are: 1) bake the bacon in the oven, so you don't have to watch it as closely and it stays soft, and 2) wash or rinse everything—utensils, bowls, etc. as soon as you can to make clean up easier."

For guests who want an extra-early breakfast, Chris offers coffee and tea, fresh squeezed orange juice and fresh fruit. She turns on her bread maker timer to start at 4:00 A.M., so a fresh loaf is ready for her guests.

HEIDI'S STUFFED FRENCH TOAST

Serves 12

1 loaf French Bread, crusts removed and cubed
16 ounces cream cheese, cubed
1 diced peach or apple
12 eggs
1/3 cup maple syrup
2 1/2 cups milk

    In a buttered or sprayed 9" X 13" baking dish layer half the bread cubes, the cream cheese cubes, the diced fruit, and the remaining bread cubes. Whisk the eggs, syrup, and milk together. Pour the milk mixture over the bread until all is thoroughly soaked. Cover and refrigerate overnight. Bake one hour at 350 degrees or until golden. This may be frozen uncooked and baked after thawing.

Gatehouse Inn
Kristi and Doug Aslin
225 Central Avenue
Pacific Grove, California 93950
telephone: (408) 649-8436

*   Kristi and Doug garnish their dishes with fresh herbs and flowers, "grown in our garden for that purpose. The herb smell is great and gives texture to the visual presentation."*

*   Early risers can prepare their own breakfasts from the well stocked guest kitchen. The Aslins keep fresh fruit, cold cereals, and yogurt for guests who want breakfast at 6:00 A.M.*

Condiments & Beverages

CINNAMON HONEY BUTTER

Makes 3 1/2 cups

CONDIMENTS AND BEVERAGES BLUE RIBBON BREAKFAST WINNER !!

4 sticks of butter
3 tablespoons cinnamon
1 1/2 cups honey

    Whip the butter and cinnamon with an electric mixer until it is light and fluffy. While the mixer is on, slowly pour the honey into the butter and blend well. Store the butter in the refrigerator in a covered container. This keeps for a long time.
    Use a melon ball tool for scooping a ball of the cinnamon honey butter on top of waffles, pancakes, and French toast. To make it easy, heat the melon ball tool in hot water.

Donna and Jerry Karson
Main Street Bed and Breakfast
403 East Main Street
Harbor Springs, Michigan 49740
telephone: (616) 526-7782

Judge's comment: "This is also great on toast, English muffins, or hot biscuits!"

HONEY PECAN BUTTER

Makes 1 1/2 cups

1/2 cup softened butter
3/4 cup pecans
1/4 cup honey

Roast the pecans at 350 degrees for 15 minutes. Grind the pecans in a food processor or blender. Add the butter and honey and mix thoroughly. Serve on pancakes or muffins. Store tightly covered in the refrigerator.

Gail Orell and Lynn Savage
Hersey House
451 North Main Street
Ashland, Oregon 97520
telephone: (503) 482-4563

When guests check in at Hersey House, Gail and Lynn find out if they have any special diet needs and what beverages they would like to drink. They discuss and finalize the menu with at this time, also.

To make clean up time easier after grinding coffee, Gail and Lynn suggest setting the grinder on a paper towel.

STRAWBERRY BUTTER

Makes 2 cups

1 stick butter
1 8 ounce package cream cheese
1/4 cup honey
1/2 cup mashed strawberries (or blueberries)

Cream the butter and cream cheese in a bowl. Add the honey and blend well. Add the mashed berries and stir until combined. Store in a covered container in the refrigerator.

MERRY BERRY SYRUP

Makes about 9 cups

4 pints strawberries, raspberries, or blueberries
2 cups sugar
1 cup lite corn syrup
1 tablespoon lemon juice

Puree the berries and pour them into a large saucepan. Add the sugar, lite corn syrup, and lemon juice and mix well. Bring the mixture to a boil. Reduce the heat to medium heat and boil, stirring occasionally, for five minutes. Skim off the foam and pour the syrup into sterilized jars. Cover and refrigerate.
This is good on pancakes, waffles, French toast, and biscuits.

The Laufersweilers recommend this syrup with their baked French toast.

Ellen and Bucky Laufersweiler
Blushing Rose Bed and Breakfast
11 William Street
Hammondsport, New York 14840
telephone: (607) 569-3402

CHERRY SAUCE

Serves 6

1 can cherry pie filling
1/4 cup white wine
1/4 cup water
3 dashes (to taste) cayenne pepper

    Bring the ingredients to a boil in a sauce pan and simmer, stirring occasionally, until the sauce is thick. This can be made ahead and reheated. Serve over hot crepes.

Rudi and Marcia Zwicker
Casa Europa Inn and Gallery
157 Upper Ranchitas Road
Taos, New Mexico 87571
telephone: (505) 758-9798

Rudi and Marcia had an unusual start one morning. "The first year we were open, we forgot to set our clock ahead in the spring for daylight savings time. We woke up at our usual time and within ten minutes had two guests sitting at the breakfast table. Somehow breakfast was prepared and served, but after that, we have been very careful to set our clock and alert our guests to the time changes."

The Zwickers have found many ways to save time in the morning. They fill the coffee makers the night before, so they just have to turn on the machine to get the morning coffee started. When making a quiche, they prebake the quiche shells and cook the vegetables for the filling the night before. In the morning, they warm the egg-milk mixture before pouring it into the quiche shell. Serving the main entree on each plate, nicely arranged and garnished, makes an efficient way to serve breakfast. They also prebake croissants the night before and pop them into the freezer. In the morning they reheat the croissants in the oven and they taste fresh baked.

RHUBARB SAUCE

Serves 8

4 cups chopped rhubarb
1/4 cup water
1 cup sugar

Cook the rhubarb and water in a saucepan over medium heat until the rhubarb is tender. Add the sugar and stir until it dissolves. This makes a good topping or side dish.

RHUBARB RASPBERRY SAUCE

Makes 4 cups

1 pound chopped rhubarb
1 10 ounce package frozen raspberries
1/2 cup sugar

Combine the ingredients in a saucepan and cook over low heat until the rhubarb is tender. Use on waffles, pancakes, and biscuits. Cover and refrigerate to store.

Ellen and Bucky Laufersweiler
Blushing Rose Bed and Breakfast
11 William Street
Hammondsport, New York 14840
telephone: (607) 569-3402

"The rhubarb raspberry sauce was a real favorite with my family," writes one judge. "We had it on our Sunday morning pancakes."

CRANBERRY CONSERVE

Makes 2 1/2 cups

1 can whole cranberry sauce
1/4 cup honey
1/4 cup raisins
1/4 cup chopped walnuts

Combine the ingredients in a microwave proof bowl. Cook on high for five minutes in the microwave. Serve warm over oatmeal.

Variations:

Make the conserve as above. Add 1/2 cup maple syrup and a jigger of brandy or sherry. This is good on French toast or pancakes.

Make the conserve as directed. Add 1/4 cup white vinegar and 1 teaspoon dry mustard for chutney.

Eileen and Jack Connell
Cape Cod Sunny Pines Bed & Breakfast Inn
P.O. Box 667
77 Main Street
Harwich West, Massachusetts 02671
telephone: (508) 432-9628

APPLE CONSERVE

Serves 12 to 15

2 quarts peeled, sliced apples
8 cups sugar
1 cup vinegar
1 cup chopped nuts

Combine the apples, sugar, and vinegar in a large pan and mix thoroughly. Cook over low heat until the apples are cooked, stirring often. Stir in the chopped nuts and remove from heat. Store in tightly covered containers in the refrigerator. Serve with toast, biscuits, or other hot breads.

> Jack and JoAnne Warmoth
> Teetor House
> 300 West Main Street
> Hagerstown, Indiana 47346
> telephone: (317) 489-4422

The judges thought this made a zesty and delicious spread for toast and warm rolls, but suggested that some cooks might choose to use a bit less vinegar.

The Warmoths remember a trying time for innkeepers. A photographer from a magazine (they so wanted to impress!) was waiting in the dining room for the Warmoths to bring in a favorite dish. As they entered the room, the food slipped off the plate and fell to the floor!

Spiced apples, apple rings, or some of their apple conserve add an extra tart garnish to the Warmoth's rich breakfast dishes. They find that make ahead casseroles help cut down on the morning rush.

RHUBARB MARMALADE

Makes 5 pints

6 cups diced rhubarb
3 cups grated raw carrot
2 medium oranges
4 1/2 cups sugar

Grate the carrots in the food processor. Wash the oranges. Chop the oranges, rind and all, in the food processor. Remove the orange seeds.

Mix all the ingredients in a large bowl and let them stand overnight.

In a large pan, cook the mixture over low heat until it begins to boil. Simmer until the marmalade thickens, about 2 hours, stirring often. Pack the marmalade in hot, sterilized jars. Process 10 minutes in a boiling water bath.

Rose Degni and Lyn Daring
Lavender Inn Bed and Breakfast
RR #1 Box 325
Seneca Turnpike East
Vernon, New York 13476
telephone: (315) 829-2440

"This makes a wonderfully mild marmalade," Rose writes, *"and uses all that rhubarb!"*

For early breakfasts, Rose and Lyn prepare muffins or a loaf of quick bread, fruit, and coffee and juice to go.

APPLE-BERRY TEA

Serves 6 to 8

8 raspberry or blackberry tea bags
2 cups boiling water
4 cups apple juice
2 teaspoons honey (to taste)

Pour boiling water over the tea bags and steep for five minutes. Remove the tea bags. Add the honey to the hot tea. Stir in the apple juice. Heat the mixture to serving temperature, but do not boil.

Karen and Jim Owens
The King's Cottage, A Bed and Breakfast Inn
1049 East King Street
Lancaster, Pennsylvania 17602
telephone: (717) 397-1017

HOT MULLED CIDER

Serves 8 to 10

2 quarts apple cider
1/2 cup brown sugar
1/2 teaspoon allspice
1 1/2 teaspoons whole cloves
2 sticks cinnamon
1/2 cup frozen orange juice concentrate

Put all the ingredients in a crock pot. Cover with the lid and simmer on low for 3 hours.

Margo Underwood
Sandlake Country Inn
8505 Galloway Road
Cloverdale, Oregon 97112
telephone: (503) 965-6745

Margo writes, "What a friendly aroma to greet our guests!"

For ordering additional copies write:
Jessica Bennett
Box 3048
Crofton, MD 21114